Faith Is: Inspiring Stories from Las Vegas Chaplains

Copyright © 2017

ISBN 978-1541242210

Cover design by Senior Chaplain Victorya

Layout and compilation by Senior Chaplain Tamia Dow

For Messages Of Faith Ministry

PO Box 60215

Las Vegas, Nevada 89160-1215

Messagesoffaith.net

messagesoffaith@juno.com

Back Cover Photo: by Senior Chaplain Dorla Stewart

Editors : Chaplains Alvin and Beverly Weesner

Advertising & Promotional Media: by Chaplain Bryan Norris

Sponsor: Senior Chaplain Marshaun AR Winston

Faith Is: The Authors

Karen R. Atlantic

Sara M. Bonaparte

Mary V. Camp

Victorya

Laquieta Cooks

Debbie Damron

Tamia Dow

Amber

Shelea A. Griffith

Barry A. Mainardi

Maria Novello

Elaine Olson

Bryan Ostaszewski

Pamela R. Poston

Walter L. Poston

Rachael Richardson

Sally St John

Dennis Smith

Leon Stevens

Kathleen Swope

Duey Vernon

Warren Vandenhoff

TABLE OF CONTENT

Faith Is: Inspiring Stories from Las Vegas Chaplains

TABLE OF CONTENT

THANK YOU

Above all to God, for His divine inspiration and provision for the completion of this Book.

I thank God and honor my Foreparents :

My Mother - Jeannette Dow

My Father - Zellie L Dow Jr (deceased)

My paternal Grandparents - Zellie & Effie Dow (deceased)

My maternal Grandparents - Nelson & Sadie Coleman (deceased)

for their inspirational lives and all their encouragement and support. They all are children of the Most High God.

No great project can be successful without the assistance of an amazing team. Our ministry is blessed with so many talented and supportive Chaplains with giant hearts of service. I am thankful for all my co-authors and their passionate love for God and His children.

Special Recognition:

Dorla Stewart, Marshaun Winston, Alvin and Beverly Weesner , DW Grant, Clark McCarrell Jr, Bryan Norris, and The LVMPD Training Department for their direction, support and assistance to the authors and the book project.

I also thank you for purchasing our book, supporting our authors & ministry and for sharing this book with your circle of influence.

May the Lord richly bless you, your life & your family. Amen.

MOFM

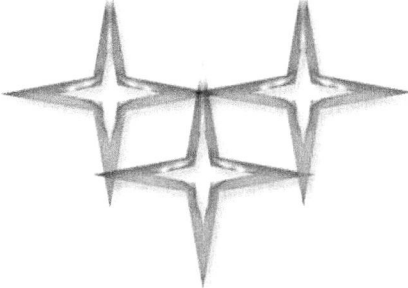

Messages of Faith Ministry

He said unto him the third time, Simon, son of Jonas, do you love me? Peter was grieved because he said unto him the third time, Do you love me? And he said unto him, Lord, you know all things; you know that I love you. Jesus said unto him, Feed my sheep.

John 21:17

FORWARD

"you know that I love you." Jesus said, "Feed my sheep"
John 21:17

The Word of God is filled with scriptures that reveal divine messages from the Father through His Son Jesus directly to all humanity for life saving purposes. For the people of this world, these messages have the power to instill a one-of-a-kind spiritual, personal relationship and communication with their Creator. God's messages are filled with hope, encouragement, love, forgiveness, instruction, and promises, which can only be achieved through faith in our Lord. Faith is trust, confidence, belief, obedience, surrender, and the willingness to follow Him wherever He may lead us, regardless of our own inabilities, and fears.

Messages of Faith Ministry is a Christian outreach located in Las Vegas, Nevada.

A Nevada State Inc. non-profit, and a federally recognized 501c3.

Messages of Faith Ministry, is also known by its acronym of "MOFM", and was founded in July 2001.

Messages of Faith is the parental umbrella Ministry over its dba's of Chaplaincy Nevada and the Nevada Chaplains Corp USA. Chaplaincy Nevada was birthed in 2007 and launched in 2009, and remains to this day the very heartbeat of MOFM, as its Chaplains Training Division. Nevada Chaplains Corp USA is the Chaplains Membership extension of the Ministry.

Chaplaincy Nevada offers its Four- Phase training program on how to become a Chaplain for Christ and community, through its Chaplains Basic, Ordination Courses, and its Anointing Ceremony. Chaplaincy Nevada also provides year round religious education, training, and discipleship through its in-house Chaplains Academy, Online Academy, and Clinical Pastoral Training earning CPE units. All trainings, materials, and instruction are provided by Chaplaincy Nevada, and are offered at no-cost to the individual. Chaplaincy Nevada trains its Chaplains in sacramental rights and ceremonies, while providing them the opportunity to also become NV State Licensed Ministers.

Messages of Faith Ministry is a pulse in the very heartbeat of Almighty God, a pulse created by God, for God, while bringing Glory to God. Chaplains volunteer and work all sectors of community as Christian "ground forces of faith" and as "boots on the ground" for all people. The sole purpose is to lift Jesus up, to be filled with the Holy Spirit, and prayerfully bring our Father in Heaven glory, all the days of our life, by stirring others to His truth, and inspiring them to Jesus Christ

We hope these stories of individual personal journeys brought to you by our Chaplains will inspire your spiritual trust to grow even more, as they offer testimonies of encouragement and hope of what,

Faith Is…

Chaplaincy

INTRODUCTION

Behind the bright lights, glitz and glamour, beyond the seductive lure of the Las Vegas strip are the people who make Las Vegas the beacon in the desert that it is.

People from around the world are drawn to Las Vegas as a Bucket list destination. It's compared to The Time Square of the west and The Tokyo of the east with 335 days of sun and more warm days then frigid. Vegas is like a well-known and misunderstood character. It's featured in many movies showing lavish scenes of decadence, greed, power and lust.

In a city world renowned for sin and darkness there are people of faith who serve the souls that are drawn to it. Like bright beacons of light they shine the way for those swallowed by the darkness. These people of faith are the men and women of the Las Vegas based Messages of Faith Ministry Chaplaincy Nevada. The team is over two hundred strong.

In this first edition of the "Faith Is…" series, you will read Chaplains stories of grace, love, hope, joy and promise that grew out of disappointments, obstacles and setbacks. These stories are told from the heart by authors who range from first-time to seasoned published authors. Each author has a unique story and a special style of sharing their lives. Their stories will encourage you, inspire you and increase your faith as you walk through their life journeys and learn from their lessons. With surrendered, willing and courageous hearts they share truths and victories. Tell the truth and shame the devil.

We welcome your thoughts, breakthroughs and the takeaways that you experience as you read through our book.

Please contact us at ChaplaincyNVbook@gmail.com with your feedback. Enjoy reading.

Senior Chaplain Tamia

Senior Chaplain Tamia Dow

Tamia is a Beloved child of God, a Woman of Faith who has served God, her community and her fellow man in many ways. She is a graduate from the University of Nevada Las Vegas with BA In Criminal Justice, a veteran of the US Army, and a retired Las Vegas Metropolitan Police Department Detective. She is an award-wining international best-selling author.

Tamia is the compiler of the "Faith Is" anthology. Her passion is empowering and educating people to live a life free from oppression and to live their life to their fullest calling. She conducts training in the area of living A God Planned Life.

Tamia does police and community outreach conducting professional and personal development training while working in the ministry of Chaplaincy. She is the Chaplain of the International Association of Women Police, a Senior Chaplain, specialty instructor and member of the Chaplain's Advisor Board with Messages of Faith Ministry Chaplaincy Nevada. www.tamiadow.com

Choosing Daily Intimacy

By Senior Chaplain Tamia Dow

"The steps of a good man are ordered by the Lord and He delights in his ways." Psalm 37:23

For years I've proudly worn a uniform. My first uniform was my uniform as a Girl Scout. The next uniform I wore was my uniform as a US Army Officer. The next uniform I wore was my uniform as a Las Vegas Metropolitan Police Department police officer. I spent 30 years in combat boots leading and training people in predominantly male careers.

As a Girl Scout, as a soldier, as a police officer, I took an oath of service. An Oath is a promise. Service is a very important core value essential to my character. All of these roles are what I call Patriot Roles, where I make a promise to live my life to protect and support my fellow man.

The Girl Scout Oath states "On my honor I will try to serve God and my country and to obey the Girl Scout Law." That may seem like a very basic oath. For me, as a little girl, it set the tone for my life. The words that stand out; Honor, God, Country.

"Train up a child in the way he should go: and when he is old, he will not depart from it." Proverbs 22:6

My mom raised my family Catholic. We were raised up to love God, the Father, Son and Holy Spirit. Service was instilled. I served while in high school and in college. I was in student council and very active in issues that mattered to my fellow classmates. The Lord has given me the Warrior Servant Leader Heart. He also instilled the knowledge to aid me in living a successful life.

God has trained me up over the years with the opportunities and challenges that sharpen my talents and increase my knowledge. I know the Lord has called me to use my life experiences and training to bless others that may not know the things I know.

God has a plan for your life and it's unique to you. It's built off of the experiences and exposures that you have had during the course of your life, and the choices that you made and make with those given circumstances. It's important that you decide whether you are going to live your God planned life or whether you are going to live your planned life. The choice is yours. The Lord has given us free will to choose whether we will do His will or whether we chase after our will.

I have not lead a perfect life. With all my accomplishments my head got big. I began to think I could do anything I wanted and that I did not need God as the lead in my life because "I Got This ". Pride and arrogance can trip up many a believer and it tripped me up many times along my path. As I look back over my life I realise that when I put Tamia first and Tamia's plans first that is when I failed, I tripped up, and I messed up because it was about me and where I felt I had gotten myself. Does this sound familiar to anyone?

Leadership is a trusted authority. When a leader moves from servant leader into more Me focused styles of leadership it opens the door to the enemy to tempt you. He came in with all kinds of temptation throughout my life and it was always with "well everyone else is doing it, what's the big deal ". I found secular mentors and modeled their leadership to my downfall.

Yet I give glory to God because He was always there with His hand extended, calling me unto Him. I am the one who stopped going to church because I did not need it. I had all I had asked for great career, new car, and a beautiful house. My job was demanding. I always felt I had to behave a certain way to fit in with "the guys".

I could curse as good as a sailor and call you all the colorful metaphors you could image to put you in line. I thought this made me tough, rugged, strong and cop-like, right?

Well that did not matter to some of my peers. I experienced something unexpected as a rookie cop, not everyone wanted me to be a cop. I know, shocking right? Well in 1989 I was only one of two black female Las Vegas Metropolitan Police Department Police Officers and I was the only one working street patrol. It's funny how I found this out. My sergeant called me in the office to talk to me about a citizen complaint. After he described the incident I asked "How do you know that was me ?" He looked at me emotionless and said "Tamia you're the only black female out here."

I was shocked. I had joined LVMPD coming from the US Army where there are countless black females serving in all aspects of the service including Military Police (my specialty). The largest police agency in Nevada only had one black female on patrol?

Being the only one made trying to fit in seem even more important yet I was struggling with my faith. A good little catholic girl who attended squad parties at bars because that's where the official debriefing of the day's work took place (telling of war stories is a form of bonding for cops). I was conflicted. I wanted to do well in my chosen career and fit in. I also knew my actions were not pleasing to God.

As a Trainee one of my Field Training Officers told me "I don't know why you're here, you are a token. You took this job from a deserving white man." Let me share something, I came to the LVMPD with US Army Military Police Officer experience and training, private security law enforcement training and a degree in criminal justice. A token I was not. I was highly qualified for the position. It hurt me to know that because I am a Black female some people may (still) feel I am undeserving of success.

14

This issue broke my heart. To the public and my colleagues I had my face set like flint, yet I was sad and discouraged everyday as I pretended to be one of the boys when I knew God was calling me to stand on my Faith. After months of stress and tears I ran to the altar. I went to a church my brother was attending and they had an altar call. They said "if you want Jesus to be your Lord and Savior come forward so that we can pray for you". I did. That was in 1990.

I immediately jumped into the Bible, studying day and night. I found comfort in the Bible, God's Word and His promises as my faith grew. I prayed for the Lord to clean up my mouth (help me stop cussing) and immediately I started choosing other words even when speaking with colleagues. They noticed the difference. I knew God had being a Law Enforcement Officer as part of His plan for my life. So I stood my ground against the naysayers and excelled in my chosen profession with God by my side. I used to say Jesus was my co-pilot riding shotgun as I patrolled the streets of Las Vegas (we work as single officer patrol units). I know He placed Angels around me and went before me on volatile situations.

Then and now I choose to focus daily on God and His plans for my life. I cannot say I am perfect. I stumbled as I have mentioned yet I want to help you be more successful in your daily path. So I share what I have learned.

"Trust in the Lord with all your heart; and lean not to your own understanding: in all your ways acknowledge Him, and He shall direct your paths."

Proverbs 3:5&6

He has given us a guidebook to direct us (the Bible). He also provides mentors and guides to help us along the way. They may come in the form of a parent, a teacher, a relative, a friend, someone from your local church or even a coworker.

Recognizing the right guides are important. Because many people come into your life saying they are there to help you, yet they're there to take you off the right path. So how do you know who is God sent and who is not?

That answer comes with your chosen daily rituals.

How is your relationship with Abba, Father?

Do you walk in daily guidance with Him, with your eyes focused on Jesus and His commandments?

If you call yourself a Christian, you are identifying yourself as a follower of Jesus Christ. If you are a follower of Christ, which means you've read the New Testament gospels, which give you instructions straight from the Messiah himself.

Have you read Matthew, Mark, Luke and John? Have you read the Acts of the Apostles?

Many people will take a lot of time to read their Facebook feed about current celebrity who are celebrities for being celebrities. They may create a You Tube channel, or be funny, or be born into a family of interest. Yet if you ask those same people questions about Jesus Christ, they would not be able to answer them. In the same series of questions, you can ask them if they consider themselves to be Christians, and they will say yes.

How can you call yourself a Christian, without having a daily relationship with Christ or knowing His teachings?

Choosing daily Intimacy will increase your faith. In this chapter, you will go through a suggested process to enable you to build your relationship with our triune God; God the father, God the son and God the Holy Spirit. Follow the steps, open your heart and you will find you have a closer relationship with God. You will also find yourself on the path to living your God planned life.

"In their hearts, humans plan their course,

but the Lord establishes their steps"

Proverbs 16:9

DAILY RITUALS

No one wakes up and says "I want to have the worst day of my life," do they?

Yet if you begin your day undirected and rushed without a solid foundation, you are releasing connection with what happens, and leaving it to the world. And I tell you, this world can be cruel. So what is a better way to start your day? Start your day with God.

Plan that first thing in the morning your daily first fruit will be given to the Lord. Why? Because we are assured in Jeremiah 29; 11:

"For I know the plans I have for you" declares the Lord.

"Plans to prosper you and not to harm you,

plans to give you hope and a future "

As soon as you wake up give Glory and Praise to God, because there are many others that did not receive God's wake up call. Their earthly journey ended yesterday or last night. If God knows the plans He has for us, should we not consult Him first before we take on any task?

We do not know when we will take our last breath. What we do know is that if the Lord sees fit for you to awaken, He wants fellowship with you.

Foundational daily rituals are keys to success.

Arise and stretch, take in fresh air to fuel your mind, body and soul. Give thanks to God, the Father, Son and Holy Spirit. Pray. Prayer is a conversation with God. Ask God to bless you, provide for you and guide you to bless others for His glory. Reflect daily on the Lord's Prayer, found in Matthew 6:9-12:

Our Father in Heaven,

Hallowed be your name.

Your kingdom come.

Your will be done

On earth, as it is in heaven.

Give us today our daily bread.

And forgive us our debts,

As we also have forgiven our debtors.

And lead us not into temptation,

But deliver us from the evil one;

For Yours is the kingdom,

And the power,

And the glory,

Forever. Amen

Devotions: Choose wisely what you read, watch or seek out for entertainment. Immerse yourself into God's Words and His teaching. You can download the Bible on your laptop, tablet and mobile phones. Websites like Bible-gateway and apps like You-Bible have daily devotionals and Bible study aids and tips. You can work your way through the Bible and, to ensure you stay true to doing it daily, you could take the Proverbs challenge and read one chapter a day, connecting to the day of the month. You read the first chapter of Proverbs on the first day of the month, Proverbs 2 on the second day of the month, Proverbs 3 on the third and so on. The Book of Proverbs has 31 chapters, so you have a chapter for each day of the month. This process helps you build up the habit of daily Bible devotions, which draws you into a closer relationship with God.

Protect your ear gates. Watch what you are listening to. Turn off negativity. What are you listening to when you're driving in the car ? From the time I was saved I began listening to Christian music stations and stopped listening to secular music, which often degraded women and glorified loose sex. I listened to a radio station called KILA 90.5FM in Las Vegas. Where Jack French was "Praising The Lord" daily. Its now called SOS Radio Sounds Of the Spirit and Jack French has passed away (RIP). It issues a 30 day challenge to new listeners to listen solely to SOS Radio for 30 days straight and watch how their spirit and outlook unto the world will change. I issue you the same challenge. If you are not in Las Vegas find the SOSRadio app on your smart phone.

Importantly Protect your eye gates. Do you really need to watch that blood and gore torture movie? or that movie about witch craft ? Or Adult Cartoons? Is that a website you should be on? What messages and images are you feeding your soul. Environment is stronger than willpower so be watchful what you surround yourself with. Remember God knows all.

"Study to show yourself approved to God,

A workmen that needs not be ashamed,

Rightly dividing the word of truth."

2 Timothy 2:15

ALWAYS BE THANKFUL

For what are you thankful?

1.   Take a minute and sit in reflective silence.
Be Still and Know that God is God!!!

2.   Look at your surroundings.

3.   Ask yourself: How has the Lord blessed me? How am I working out God's plan for my life? What am I doing with the Time, Talents and Abilities God has blessed me with?

4.   Write out the responses to these questions.

5.   Create a gratitude list from your responses.

If you woke up this morning and are reading this book - Be Thankful.

If you have people who love and care for you, people who support you and help you through life - Be Thankful.

If you can go outside and smell the fresh air, see the sky, stretch and move your body without pain (and even with pain because pain signals us that we need to address something within us) - Be Thankful.

If you ask "Chaplain, how can I be thankful if my body is in pain or I am in a wheel chair or recovering from an injury?"

I answer, "Because thankfully you are here to live another day; to interact with your loved ones and to make a difference in this world."

Study the parable of the talents. (Matthew 25:14-30) God has given each of us according to our abilities. How have you been using your talents? Are you multiplying them or leaving them buried? What will you have to present to the Master when He returns?

Life is 10% what happens to us and 90% how we choose to respond to it. Our response is our choice. We have a high calling on our lives. We are Royalty, children of the King of Kings and Lord of Lords. Our lives are not perfect, yet we can live the lives we have been given with an attitude of thankfulness and share our gratitude with the people we influence. We influence people we may never meet or who may never tell us we influenced them. We must be aware. Someone is Always Watching what we choose to do.

Live your life in integrity. Choose God Daily.

Senior Chaplain Victorya

Victorya is the Founder of Messages of Faith Ministry and its Chaplaincy Nevada division. She is the volunteer Academy training program and development operations executive director. She has been a published Christian Author since 2005. In 1998 she had a face-to-face encounter with Christ. She is a Nevada State Licensed Minister. Victorya is a Prayer Invocator for Clark County and the City of Las Vegas. In 2015 she was awarded Lifetime Achievement Recognition for her work from the NV State Governors Office, US Senatorial, US House of Representatives, US House of Congress, and partnered organizations. She has worked in conjunction with Nevada educational entities since 1995. She retired from her choice of sports in TaeKwonDo martial arts in 2007 as a 4th degree black belt, referee, and judge. She is the mother of four.
www.messagesoffaith.net

The Mustard Seed

By Senior Chaplain Victorya

Truly I tell you, if you have faith as small as a mustard seed, you can say to this mountain, 'Move from here to there,' and it will move. Nothing will be impossible for you. Matthew 17:20

The sun is beginning to set; the day is drawing nigh, and two hrs. later I find myself still sitting in the same chair quietly looking out the window; with continued thoughts and a focus on the very essence of life's "trials and tribulations". The journey has been long-suffering, the storms filled with heartache, and yet I knew through all of the hardships that the sovereign hand of God is always in control. The passage of time has not only taught me, but also changed me from that person I once was and into to the person I am today. Only by the sheer mighty will of Gods divine providence and grace was it completed. Faith is agreeing to that small spiritual incision, that tiny heartfelt mustard-seed size of an opening, which allows the Spirit of God his entrance to work within us, while nurturing and filling us with godly and divine revelation.

Looking back through the years in my journey of life there is only one obvious answer that has brought me forward to this day, and the answer is unequivocally without a doubt known as "faith". Faith for me is revealed and grows on a daily basis through my relationship with Jesus Christ. Faith is so very important because it grants me that strong confident trust in the Lord, even when the trials of life are on the attack and heavily abound.

Faith, trust, confidence, obedience and my love for Jesus has enabled me through the years to walk-the-walk through the heat of the fire, to endure the raging storm, to tread every valley, to climb every inch of the mountain, and to break the chain of bondage that held the penalty of death over me. How was that possible? The answer lies in truth, and the truth is I was Chosen to be His from the very beginning of my existence.

This is my true story and testimony, a memory of a very vivid time when Jesus literally showed up in my life, a moment that time cannot erase. I ask, was it a vision, a manifestation, an encounter? Call it whatever we will, the truth is He is very real, very alive, and suddenly here he was standing next to me, and He was speaking directly to every fiber of my being.

The following is an excerpt from my book; Chosen, 15 Minutes with Jesus, published in 2011.

I know the ones I have chosen John 13:18

"There is no explanation that I can offer to the reader for the divine visitation, and eyewitness event I received from Jesus Christ; which changed this into the most important night of my life. The time I spent with Him during the manifestation miracle froze time, and yet if I had to make an educated guess on the visited length of time according to our conversation, then my best guess would be, 15 minutes with Jesus.

The conversation, the question he asked, the revelation of what is most important to Him will forever be etched in my heart and mind, in the reality and consciousness of that visitation. The time spent with Jesus changed my life, and from that moment on nothing would ever be the same.

I don't know why Jesus chose to visit me; I'm not extraordinary, wealthy, or sinless. Of all the patriarchs written in the Old Testament, I find myself most in awe, and reflective of David. King David was a warrior, he slayed a giant to protect, he fought for what he believed was the righteousness of God, and there wasn't any person who could change his mind. David battled, he went to war, and many who pretended to befriend him really despised him. Although he went through trials and fears, he always went forward. He made mistakes; he sinned, yet always praised God. Now God would punish David when he saw it necessary, yet he forgave him through his repentance. Through all my battles, wars, and sins, God has also chosen to forgive me, through my repentance. Why?

I felt overwhelmed and bitter, I was going through a very stressful period, and the time was approximately January of 1998. I was in a bitter court battle with my daughter's father; and it seemed to be a never ending battle with him, and his wife. I was facing them with both their attorneys from California and Las Vegas.

A few years earlier in a dream I stood in the light and felt the presence of God, but yet another presence was nearby, that of a mother, it was Mary. I could feel their presence from nearby, and I turned my head slowly to the left to look at them. I heard His voice say to me *turn back around; it's not your time, go back.* No, I answered. This feeling within me was far too beautiful and I wanted to look at Him and see Him, and maybe even to feel Him. Again he spoke, *turn around go back.* I did not want to.

I asked why? Who would want to leave this heavenly realm of

peace and joy? He spoke, *your children need you, go back.* No, I want to stay; I don't want to go back! Then he showed me their faces, two girls and a boy; the faces of my children. *Go back he said, your children need you.* I opened my eyes, and it was morning.

I would go through hell the next few years trying to rear two teenage girls. They were proving to be much like their mother at that age, and I couldn't have that. I had kept them busy over the years with dance, modeling and martial arts. They were determined to rebel; they had a chip on their shoulders because of their parent's relationship. Through days, months and even years I put my faith and trust in God to help me get my kids through life. To many days of depression, heartbreak and tears, I felt as if I was losing a battle.

My sister Connie was of no help to me; she was busy introducing my girls to her friends and their drugs. I needed to put on the full armor of battle. There were days I felt I was in a battle with satan himself over their lives, and I would be damned if I was going to lose one hair on their heads to the evil of drugs, or death. I placed my faith in God, and God promised that my child with an addiction would be returned. I saw a brief vision of her in a military uniform and then suddenly the vision was gone.

For two long years I would battle over the drug addiction in her life, and she looked as if she were on deaths door. The day my brother died was the day her life changed. He was a father figure to both girls; in his death her life would be regenerated. She beat the addiction, and just as in the brief vision God had showed me, she entered the military. My older daughter was married and had two sons. I felt at ease, as if these specific battles were won.

In January of 1998 my brother Frank was accompanying me to California for a court appearance. During the drive we began talking about religion, he asked me if I had ever heard of, or watched Pat Robertson. I answered no why? He said, you might want to check him out too. One night I was up late and decided to check out CBN as he suggested. I wasn't sure what I thought of the show, these people were having revelations and this was a bit much for me. I changed the channel. During the next couple of weeks I would find myself going back to their show also known as the 700 Club, and I was still not sure what I thought. My Catholic background and upbringing seemed to prevent me from accepting this type of act of "healing" so easily. I had to ask, were these people strange? Or was it just me?

It was late and I was ready to relax and watch some television, hoping it would make me tired enough to pop off to sleep. The 700 Club was on again, somehow I managed to switch it on while playing with the remote. Gordon Robertson was talking, convincing people in his audience about Jesus and his saving grace. He then asked people to pray with him. Gordon was saying that "Jesus could manifest and reveal himself" to us if we would trust him.

I thought this was strange because this meant to "unveil by sight" and therefore he must be mistaken in what he was saying or he just wasn't presenting his belief correctly. He asked again for people to believe, because Jesus could show up in their life. Okay I asked, what was this and was it possible? I answered my own question, well yes, all things are possible with God, and I would leave it at that. Pray with me, he asked again. Okay I thought, I will pray with you, after all what could it hurt and who would know, besides I was all alone in the room and there was no one to call me ridiculous.

I opened my eyes from the prayer and looked down towards my feet, what was happening, my toes felt prickly. Then the tingling began and became stronger and it began moving up my feet to my ankles, and then to my knees. The sensation transformed itself into a warm wave of rushing water flowing from within me. My eyes traveled up my body alongside the warm billowing feeling which had now made its way up to my chest. Oh my God what was happening? Upward, until I felt the wave touch the top of my head, and then an explosion of light was everywhere.

I had been lifted; I was in the middle of the brightest, whitest light I had ever seen. I felt him, and then I saw him from the corner of my right eye. I began turning my head slowly to the right until I was looking directly at him. He was here, fully. I looked, and saw him standing next to me. The light was as white as snow and it was protruding from his chest, it was so bright I could not see his eyes, yet I knew who he was. He spoke, "Can You Forgive"?

I stared at him, then he raised his right hand and stretched out his arm, I followed the length of his arm, his hand seemed to be pointing toward something. I looked over and directly in front of me was what looked like a projection screen. Then again he asked, "Can You Forgive"?

I looked back at the screen. Images began to form and suddenly the faces of my daughter's father and his wife appeared. I sat staring at them as my mind contemplated his question. Then with a shrug I said yes, my answer was yes, I could forgive. Behind them another face appeared, I stared at the face of my father and again I answered yes. Then suddenly tiny bubbles were popping up all over the screen, there were so many faces that I did not recognize them all, again my answer was yes.

At that moment something shot through me, exhilaration, ecstasy, peace, love and over-whelming joy. The feeling was as if rockets had gone off, fireworks of extra-ordinary proportions; light as white as snow and rainbows of many colors. I was soaring upwards, I looked down and saw my feet beneath me and below my feet I saw the earth and it was falling fast away from me.

I felt him, I heard him say, "nothing matters, what is of the earth and the world stays of the earth and world, work, struggle, strife, sorrow, blame, anger, unforgiveness, materials, and sin. The only thing that matters is God". Everything was falling away from me, all of the burdens and weight were being lifted from me and suddenly I realized, God is the only answer, the only one who matters, it is to Him we owe our life and loyalty, now and forever.

I was suspended in light and everlasting joy, and then suddenly I looked over and I thought this isn't normal. I looked back at Jesus, and asked am I dying? "No", and just as suddenly as he appeared, he was gone. I was still sitting on my bed, the television was still on the program and Gordon Robertson was saying to the audience, if you just prayed that prayer then call us and let us know that you prayed with us today.

I sat there in absolute amazement for a moment. Oh my God! What just happened? But I knew in my heart what had just happened. When I was very young I prayed to the Virgin Mary and waited for her to appear to me, she never did. God went further than my prayer in His grace, and God had another plan for me. God showed up, and showed me how much He loved me. The Father wanted me to meet his Son, the Resurrection of Life. God had just introduced me to His Son Jesus, and Jesus Christ was alive. *Victorya ©2011*

The Lord found a surrender of will within me, an opening the size of a Mustard-seed, and He planted His seed firmly in my heart to take root, and to grow. The seed sprouted and blossomed into an unimaginable fertile vine of ripened fruit, which bore an unalterable faith in Him. The results have changed my life, all stemming from the willingness to say yes, to accept and to receive Him. Imagine just for a moment, the possibilities He can do with you, if you give Him just a Mustard-seed size chance to plant the truth, and faith within you.– Faith Is…

He presented another parable to them, saying, "The kingdom of heaven is like a mustard seed, which a man took and sowed in his field; and this is smaller than all other seeds, but when it is full grown, it is larger than the garden plants and becomes a tree, so that the Birds of the Air come and Nest in its Branches.
Matthew 13:31-32

Senior Chaplain Laquieta Cooks

Chaplain LaQuieta Cooks is a wife, mother, grandmother and minister of the gospel. She has a heart for the word of God and relies solely on God as her source for everything she needs. Her prayer and passion is for the body of Christ to demonstrate the Love & Unity of Christ; with expectancy for the glory and power of God, to be seen to the entire world. She has a Bachelors Degree in the study Theology, through Minnesota School of Theology, a Graduate of Sonship School of The First Born through Destiny Christian Center, she is an Ordained Senior Chaplain with Messages of Faith Ministry; where she also serves as a Advisory Board Member, Academy & CPE Instructor. Chaplain LaQuieta is a licensed minister & partner at Destiny Christian Center, serving in the ministry of Preaching, Teaching, Altar Worker & Discipleship. As an Ordained Chaplain, LaQuieta also minister's to Gods precious young people that are incarcerated at Clark County Detention Center & Juvenile Detention Center. In her 37 years of marriage, to Chaplain Charles, God has lovingly blessed them as one; together, they share the word of God & their marriage testimony. They are both anointed with a specific focus and passion to restore hope, faith and the expectation of Unity & Love in Marriages and Families; believing God, that this will have a direct impact on the Body of Christ, manifesting his word & glory! (Matthew 17:21-23 & Psalms 133:1-3)

Marriage "From Ashes to Beauty"

By Senior Chaplain Laquieta Cooks

Isaiah 61:3
"to give unto them beauty for ashes, the oil of joy for mourning, the
garment of praise for the spirit of heaviness; that
they might be called trees of righteousness, the planting of the Lord,
that he might be glorified."

Faith is the expressed confidence in receiving God's promises, even though I don't see them. Faith is, holding fast to, and resting upon every word in *Psalms 91*.

After years of adultery plaguing my marriage, and my focus being why, how long, and all the other particulars (according to my emotions and self absorbed soul); God spoke to my heart, asking, "When will you really trust me with this matter"?

That day I surrendered myself and my marriage to God; I repented, and received God's word for me concerning the matter that lingered over me, and deep within my heart. At this place in my life, confusion and doubt tormented me as I contemplated between trusting God, or just to simply get a divorce. Although I was saved and believed in God, I lacked the knowledge of how to activate Faith, and the power that was available to me by having Faith in Christ.

My mindset of thinking that I could handle this matter myself and my way, only made things worse. With every attempt to fix and resolve this issue (doing things my way!), my prayer life decreased, I lost sight of Gods righteousness; thereby, entering into a downward spiral of self pity, loneliness, danger and anger.

First things, First! Stay engaged with prayer; accelerate your faith.
When it seems hopeless, impossible and quite unfair, "pray without
ceasing" and feed your faith (speak the word only!)

Faith is, To Surrender. I had to learn how to surrender; to surrender everything that aileth me, and my marriage had become a thing that aileth me. I believed in God and I love God; but my words and behavior, announced and displayed a lack of trust. Once I surrender my marriage to God; my marriage became my container of hope! My "now faith" in the living word of God became the substance of what I hoped and believe for my marriage. I couldn't see the blessings of God in or for my marriage; but, through faith, it became evident!

My Heavenly Father caused is goodness to rain down and manifest, according to His ordained creation for marriage. News Flash!...God specializes in the impossible. Faith is knowing and trusting that the substance of the word is sufficient to fuel & maintain my container of hope. I've been married for 37 years; the first year, all the romance my heart desired, splendid - heaven on earth! Year two - betrayal by adultery; year three - betrayal by adultery; how will we ever get through this? Why me? What did I do to deserve this? I thought you loved me! During the first 17 years of marriage, we faced, seven different attacks of adultery. Let's not forget about the side effects of adultery (guilt, shame, blame, lying, bitterness, anger, denial, shattered trust, etc.); and the effects it has on the family, especially the children.

Faith Is, Standing Firm.
Faith is knowing that the power of God prevails; the power of God prevails in the darkness of the midnight hour, the power of God prevails when everything, based on the surrounding and taunting circumstances seems hopeless; the power of God prevails even when it feels as though your heart has been torn to pieces. When the shame of adultery, causes you to sink into despair, and convinces you that there's no one to confide in, and that no one cares or understands; God cares and His power will prevail! Often, in this valley of darkness, I experienced thoughts and moments of being

33

exiled (taken away from what I knew to right and good). My way of
life, and doing things, all changed; yet, I had made the choice to trust
God. I continued to live and rejoice in God, building myself up on
His most holy word; because He is "a very present help"
(*Psalms 46:1-2*).

With every day of testing, I leaned on and trusted God more. I
learned to hold on to the hand of God, trusting Him to restore all that
had been ruined, broken and burned. When others said, "you'll never
have complete trust in your marriage again", I remembered God's
words to me, "to trust Him"; I spoke the word, believed the word;
God is faithful, and, "the prayers of the righteous availeth much".
God created marriage, ordained marriage, gave specific instructions
for and in marriage, then sealed it "(let no man put asunder
what God has joined...)"

Today, right now, your marriage may be in ruins. The task of
trusting your spouse, rebuilding all that's been destroyed, and
continuing in your marriage, may look and appear to be an
"impossible mission" and overwhelming; but, "all things are possible
through Christ", and" greater is He, that lives in you; that places you
in the winning position! "Faith is the evidence, of things not seen".
Certainly, others are questioning your commitment to your marriage,
making comments that it will never be the same, your spouse will
never change, cut your ties, and God will bless you with someone
else, someone better. Seek wise counsel (*Proverbs 19:21*)!
1 Corinthians 7:12 "But to the rest speak I, not the Lord:..."
*1 Corinthians 7:15-16 MSG "On the other hand, if the unbelieving
spouse walks out....."*

The above scriptures, in there entirety, speaks to both the believer
and the nonbeliever (God has a plan). Faith is...my trust in God, and
my faith in His word. My Father's love for me has caused me to
know that I am valuable to Him, and that I am so much more than
my circumstances. As His children, we have the blessed assurance in
knowing, that by Faith, in-spite of the good, the bad and the ugly, the
power of God prevails and we are more than a conqueror, we are
over-comers.

Faith is a quiet soul in the Storms of life.

God Is my Comforter! Do you know Him as your Comforter? When things are not as we wish, and the resonating sound of your heart being broken, echoes louder, with each and every passing minute, God is our Comforter; deeply troubled from every angle, and distracted by our pain, God is our Comforter. Faith is expecting the Spirit of God to comfort you with His peace; peace that flows to each us like a river, as Christ Jesus breathes upon us and says, "Peace be unto you." Do you know and possess that peace? Faith is enjoying God's heavenly calm—when pain & circumstances should have distracted you. Faith in God, leads us to a place of rest in Jesus. The comfort of the Holy Spirit takes the sting and bitterness out; it quiets our souls in Gods' "peace that surpasses all understanding" (*Psalms 57:1, Philippians 4:7*). God is faithful in times of trouble and His mercy endures forever. We are never alone! In the darkest night, the deepest valley, even under the weight of our circumstances, God will quiet our hearts and give us confidence to be and remain faithful to Him.

Faith Is Pleasing.

Faith is choosing to believe the report of the Lord! Faith is" what it takes to please our God. Choose to believe God! Our God is a "a God that cannot lie"! Our God is Faithful and He will redeem your time. My Marriage is a faithful testimony, of Gods faithfulness to perform His word, manifest His power, love, goodness, mercy and grace. My choice to walk by faith, to believe and trust God, is the only reason I am victorious and blessed in my marriage; faith is how, I overcame every side effect (Insecurity, Anger, Bitterness, Distrust, etc.) that occurred as a direct result of the adultery.

I encourage every reader of this chapter, to walk confidently in your "now faith! Faith is pleasing unto God! So, Believe God for an Honorable Marriage; believe God, to perform *Isaiah 61:3. No* matter what you're going through or how it looks, God is faithful, and He's watching over His word to perform it.
"To appoint unto them that mourn in Zion, to give unto them beauty for ashes, the oil of joy for mourning, the garment of praise for the spirit of heaviness; that they might be called trees of

righteousness, the planting of the Lord, that he might be glorified."
It doesn't matter what it currently looks like, what others say, think
or believe; what does the word of God say? Who's report do you
believe? Faith is following the prescribe prescription for a life that
mirrors the life of Christ, and pleasing to our Heavenly Father; "for
without faith, it is impossible to please God". We must learn and
discipline our minds to think on those things that lovely and true.

Faith Is The Power of God.
I had to learn to believe God in every area of my life, at all times, no
matter the cost. The cost of being called crazy, told I was in a state
of denial, even delusional. Don't get me wrong, there was a time,
when I was all of those things; even while I yet professed Christ as
my Lord & Savior; I lived a saved, but powerless life ("Saved, but
defeated"). Although Saved, the defeat was deeply embedded in my
heart & mind, because of all the defeating words, that others
spoke and those words I spoke from my mouth. ("We have the
power of life or death in our tongue"). Nothing is to hard for God!
What appeared impossible to me & others, became an opportunity
for God. Faith is yielding to God's word, His way, speaking His
word about the matter, taking hold of the duty of Faith; living as
though it's already done! "Faith is the substance of things hoped for,
the evidence of things not seen". God taught me to see my husband
& marriage, through His eyes (His Word, whose report will you
believe?)

The marriage my family, friends & others see today, is the making of
God; chiseled, refined, restored and orchestrated by the loving hands
of God. Faith was and is the substance of my hope! While we wait,
we wait in faith, with expectation according to Ephesians 3:20. God
created and ordained marriages; God called me first, to be a servant,
that obeys His word, no matter what (No Matter What!!); then He
gently corrected and taught me to be a wife. (He is the author and
finisher). Jesus made disciples and he called for disciples to go and
make more disciples (I see more godly marriages). Just like He made
disciples, healed the sick, restored sight to the blind, turned water
into wine; Undoubtedly, God has the power to restore and make
godly marriages.

My marriage is the making of God; through tears, through humility, through shame, and anger, Faith is knowing that God is not only able, but faithful to complete:

 "Whatever God has promised gets stamped with the Yes of Jesus. In him, this is what we preach and pray, the great Amen, God's Yes and our Yes together, gloriously evident. God affirms us, making us a sure thing in Christ, putting his Yes within us. By his Spirit he has stamped us with his eternal pledge—a sure beginning of what he is destined to complete." (*2 Corinthians 1:20-22 MSG*)

Faith is, "Not My Past".
God is my help, and yours for today; our hope for the future (*Psalms 27:1*). If we believe and have faith, we have access to an unwavering confidence in God which neutralizes all fear and loneliness. Faith is not our past hurts, sins, nor the past sins of our spouse!" Therefore if any man be in Christ, he is a new creature: old things are passed away; behold, all things are become new." (*2 Corinthians 5:17*) "looking unto Jesus the author and finisher of our faith; who for the joy that was set before him endured the cross, despising the shame, and is set down at the right hand of the throne of God". (*Hebrews 12:2*) Trust the Helper! When your heart aches, and you feel as though you can barely breath, because the weight of the pain is so heavy upon you chest/heart, keep believing, keep trusting, hold fast and know that our God is faithful in your faithfulness to believe. God is making "beauty from your ashes", He's creating within you, "Unmovable Faith" and "Unspeakable Joy".

Growing in Faith.
"And beside this, giving all diligence, *add to your faith* virtue; and to virtue knowledge; and to knowledge temperance; and to temperance patience; and to patience godliness; and to godliness brotherly kindness; and to brotherly kindness charity. For if these things be in you, and abound, they make you that ye shall neither be barren nor unfruitful in the knowledge of our Lord Jesus Christ." (*2 Peter 1:5*) While learning the word & will of God regarding marriage, God changed me! My marriage became that of great importance to me, because I now have an understanding of the importance of marriage

to my Heavenly Father from His perspective. But, recently, because our faith must be consistently growing, God spoke to my heart, and said "its now time for you to be a Godly wife, through my eyes, and not your eyes". This, of course, requires faith, (here I'am thinking, it can't get any better than this); *"For my thoughts are not your thoughts, neither are your ways my ways, saith the Lord, Isaiah 55:8".* A godly Marriage is a reflection, of our Heavenly Fathers desired relationship, between Him and each of His children, and to display the love of Christ to and for a lost world.

My Faith & God's Faithfulness.
Because of God's faithfulness, I'm embarking upon the enlargement of a heart with an "Attitude of Gratitude"; a heart of continuous thanksgiving; always remembering Gods grace, mercy and blessings to me. A heart that sees and finds ways to thank, honor and please God in every moment of life.

Faith is, my marriage, your marriage, whatever trial you may be facing, God is looking for your faith, and ready to turn your "Ashes to Beauty". Although, at times, I initially thought and made this thing of adultery, to be about me; I learned, that it was never just about me. It was far---bigger than just me! However, I would and did benefit from the good that would come out it; it was all about the "Kingdom of God" ("that we might be called trees of righteousness, the planting of the Lord, that he might be glorified").

"N.O.W. Faith Is,"
Not Overwhelmed or Wavering

Senior Chaplain Debbie Damron

Debbie is an ordained and Nevada State licensed Chaplain. She is an active Chaplains Advisory Board Member. She is a LVMPD METRO Volunteer, and METRO RECAP Volunteer. Debbie is the Lead Chaplain ministering the Biblical Studies program inside CCDC for certified incarcerated juveniles. Debbie has been certified in various fields including, Conflict Resolution, Suicide Prevention and Alertness, Domestic Violence Awareness, CPR, First Aid, Community Emergency Response Team Training, FEMA Emergency Preparedness, Human Trafficking, Abuse, Neglect, and Exploitation of Children and /or the Elderly, and a SNCGTF Gangs Lead. Debbie has received the Senatorial Certificate of Congratulations in Honor and Recognition of her participation in the Hope for Prisoners Re-entry Mentor Certification Training. She received a Certificate of Appreciation from the State of Nevada Office of the Governor in recognition as a Nevada Volunteer. http://www.chaplaincynevada.org/Advisory-Board.html

Who Else But God

By Senior Chaplain Debbie Damron

Faith Is believing "who else but God" could either use me, or any of my own personal life situations for His divine intervention. The story I'm about to reveal has taught me the true understanding of surrender, by allowing God to use me as his instrument in the process of introducing and experiencing a new global relationship, and a lasting friendship with a young man from Uganda. The Lord touched my heart, and has allowed my faith to grow in Him by giving me a greater understanding. This reality has clearly shown me how big the God I serve truly is.

In him we were also chosen, having been predestined according to the plan of him who works out everything in conformity with the purpose of his will, Ephesians 1:11

Looking back, I realize that God can use any situation we are in for his glory. In 2014, I found myself struggling with physical afflictions and limited mobility from back, and knee injuries. Most of the time I was following the doctors' orders for bed-rest, as my surgery dates were being scheduled. Needless to say, feeling bedridden, I had quite a bit of time on my hands, and tended to utilize social media quite a bit. One day in particular, I checked into my Facebook account and saw a friend request from a young man by the name of Fred W., who lives in Uganda. Fred and I became friends, and spent the next two years getting to know one another, learning about our families, cultures, and faith in Christ. The more I learned of this young man, the more I learned the depth of the poverty he resided in, and the more our friendship grew, the more I felt the Holy Spirit at work in this long distance friendship.

I found it was hard for me to form the notion that this humble spirited young man of faith who lived in such poverty, believed, without any doubt, that prayer and fasting were his keys to overcoming everything. We take so much for granted here at home, that when discussing the level of his poverty and enormous faith, it could only inspire my faith in God to grow even more. Fred shared that he lived in a one-room house, and ten other villagers shared the bathroom he and his family used. Although Fred and his wife Rebecca cook in their one room home, they have the opportunity to cook with others in what he called a "store", where all cooking is done by coal, and limited cooking utensils.

When I first met Fred, he had only one daughter by the name of Blessing, who was one year old. I remember asking Fred if Blessing owned any dolls, in which he informed me that she did not. I suddenly felt heartbroken over this, but I knew they could not afford to buy her a baby-doll. I felt the need for this child to be gifted a doll, which lay heavy on my heart, and I wanted to send her one. Unfortunately, neither Fred nor I knew too much about the international mailing services for sending such a gift to his country, much less his village, but I believed that God could find a way for making this happen.

In the beginning of our friendship, I learned that Fred was assisting in preaching at his church. He informed me that in 2009 he heard from the Lord in a prophetic way, and the message was to become an Apostle. He felt an overwhelming power of transformation, and began to evangelize in college and the nearby towns. This was the beginning of his Christian mission. In Uganda, the believer can be met with extreme persecution, coming from village witch doctors, and even from other professed believers. Fred pushed on in faith.

During the growth of our friendship, back here at home a dear friend had passed away suddenly, and I would be attending his Celebration of Life service. At the service I ran into a dear friend of mine, Vacheral, who was a leader with Y-WAM (Youth with a Mission) and I asked her when, and where she would be going on her next mission. I couldn't believe it when she told me the upcoming mission would be to an orphanage in Uganda, and she would be flying directly into Kampala where Fred lived.

I was so excited to hear this news, and I immediately asked if she could take little Blessing's gift to her, as I was determined to have Blessing own her very own baby-doll. My friend smiled and said yes, she would be happy to deliver the gift. God is good! My daughter and I went shopping to find Blessing a doll and other small gifts for the family. My friend received the gifts and she was able to fit them in her luggage to deliver to Fred and his family. Around this time Fred asked permission to call me Mom. It was an endearing and emotional welcome.

When all possibilities come from God, I call that Divine intervention. I would never have imagined that the next mission's stop on their itinerary would be in the same country and town where my newfound friends lived in. When I informed Fred of this amazing news he became so excited that he immediately wanted to host the Missions team that consisted of eleven females, teenage and adult, in his home. Fred asked for my advice on what he should make available for the visit, as he was very limited on funds. Due to his insistence, we decided fresh fruit and water would suffice, as the team wasn't expecting anything back from the visit. Fred and his family met the team at the airport and gracefully received the gifts, and acknowledged the team with delight. The team was also invited to speak at church, which was followed by the invitation to Fred's family home. The team accepted.

A proud Rebecca played hostess to the team by setting a humble, yet beautiful table of fresh fruit and drinks, and they managed to find enough chairs for all to sit. Rebecca entertained the team with wonderful stories of how she and Fred met, and about their life. My friend was able to capture the amazing grace in the pictures she took of this heartwarming visit. As a friend and as a courtesy, she posted the pictures online for me, so I could partake in this incredible journey and joy. Once she returned back home, she surprised me with printed copies of the trip. In my heart-of-hearts I know that only God could have made this happen.

After the YWAM visit, Fred's landlord then paid him a visit, all the while insisting that he must have received money from this team of "white people". At this time Fred's home did not have electricity. This is when I learned, although the cost of living was extremely inexpensive, a man's earnings and monthly paycheck was very nominal, and could barely accommodate the cost of living for them. Fred and Rebecca are an educated couple, who had received scholarships to attend college. To earn a scholarship, a person had to show merit of high intelligence as well as grades.

Fred was currently working construction for a man that didn't seem interested in paying his workers their full amount, or if he chose, not at all. Fred was struggling with this as he needed his pay, but he had difficulty in relaying this to his boss and others, due to his feeling of embarrassment over it. When we did speak about this situation, he told me he that he hadn't been paid for three weeks, yet he didn't want to leave because the boss kept telling him he would be paid. Fred and I continued to pray about this, and around the 4th week he said, "you know, Mom, God told me it was time for me to go and be a Pastor, but strangely I haven't been paid since I heard that." I believe Fred hears from God, he prays fervently and fasts, and goes to where he calls "Prayer Mountain" in his village. After careful consideration, his thoughts were that he should have listened to God when he told him this, not when he decided it was time.

Fred decided to work one more week and then talk to his boss again

about his back-pay; it didn't completely work out. However, he did receive a portion of the pay. Fred knew he had to quit this job and listen to what God was telling him, even though he had no idea how he would feed his family. What Fred did know was by faith and trusting in God, everything would work out accordingly. Fred then went up to Prayer Mountain, praying and fasting, and the Lord was faithful. The Lord told Fred to build a prayer altar, and to pick the location, so he decided to build it in his one room home. The town's people heard of this and began coming to his home for prayer.

Meanwhile back at home, I met an evangelist Missions Pastor by the name of Jock, who was speaking at my church. After the service I quickly introduced myself. In the short conversation, I gave him the information of Fred and the YWAM organization. We then scheduled a time to meet and discuss this further. We met and became instantly connected in friendship. I believe this to be another divine intervention, as he is now a spiritual mentor for Fred and his family.

My new Missions friend informed me that he felt led by the Spirit to help finance Fred for one year, due to the loss of his income, and while concentrating on his studies for becoming a Pastor. During this time, Fred's own Pastor removed him from his church for fear of losing his own congregation to Fred, showing no interest that Fred was following the Lords instruction.

As Fred's ministry was growing, he heard God say to him, "Have a conference in your own home village" where his extended family lived. He went forward in obedience, based on trust without any finances to help him. The conference was a success. Fred then heard God say to him, "start a church, its time." This confirmed to Fred what he had already been thinking of and planning, as he was already looking for church locations. In 2016, the Lord revealed to Fred the church was to be named, "Jesus for All Nations Restoration Ministries" and so the work began. The location he picked for the church was right next door to the police station. In this impoverished land, most village churches have dirt floors, and constant construction on them is on-going. They are constructed with sheet metal on top and sides, and the wood seems more like mere twigs. With a small donation they went from renting twenty chairs to purchasing them. Eventually, they were also able to purchase a cable to provide power. I am filled with emotions of encouragement, hope and thankfulness at being a part of this journey, it overwhelms me with gratitude and new found faith in humanity.

When I shared with my friends at home about Fred's mission they became impressed with this young man. Many of them went to social media and added him as their friends, opening new relationships for Fred and his family. Fred's only pair of shoes were very worn and tattered. My friend, Angel, sent him a donation which he used to purchase not one but two new pairs of shoes. He was so overcome with thankfulness that he named one pair of shoes Angel, and the other pair of shoes Sanchez. I am so grateful to my friends Marshaun, Blanca and Evelyn for believing in Fred's faith and work in the Lord, which compelled them to help support Fred with small donations to help advance this new church. They realized the support they gave wasn't really based on money, but rather their faith in the Lords work through this young man in the town of Kampala, Uganda.

During this time Rebecca became pregnant, and gave birth to a beautiful baby girl. Fred asked me if I would name the baby either after myself or after my own daughter, Devoney; he made the choice mine. Fred and Rebecca's new daughter was named Angelique, after my daughter's middle name. Angelique Patience made her way into the world on August 15th 2016.

Fred's story is far from finished. I know that God has so much more in store for our friendship, a friendship that reaches across borders, and oceans to embrace. As I mentioned before, we serve a big God; He sets our time, our seasons, and our paths in life. The Lord has taught me about divine intervention, that all things are possible, even when you're not expecting it. There are no coincidences in the lives of the believers, especially when so many connect in one place that spans the globe, so far apart, yet so close. I am so blessed to know, to follow, and to see this young man of 28 yrs. have the amount of faith that he does through all of his obstacles. It has given me unimaginable faith to trust in the Lord each time another connection happens.

Pastor Fred's church continues to grow, as he continues to grow in the Lord. I feel truly blessed to be a part of it all. This is a family who has yet to understand the freedoms and enjoyment we take for granted here at home. For Fred's family one of the very few times they have been able to shop together, to enjoy a family outing, and to bless little Blessing with a treat, was to visit the town and have a family ice cream sit down. It's hard for me to imagine living this way. One way for me to give back and show my gratitude is to send small gifts that are cherished, and surprisingly, to go further than I expected. I believe this young man is truly anointed by God, and will someday speak all over Uganda. My God-size dream is that the Lord will provide Fred and his family a way to travel to the US, and to speak at my church.

Faith believes in something you can't see or touch but you know it is there. My love for this young family and the friends who have helped along the way is tremendous. This friendship continues on with prayer and guidance from the Holy Spirit. Faith is the Lord's hand working in me, for Uganda.

But God...

Matthew 7:7 Ask and it will be given to you, seek and you will find, knock and the door will be open to you.

Senior Chaplain Barry Mainardi

Chaplain Barry graduated from the University of Dayton, served with the U.S. Army and received an Honorable Discharge at the rank of Captain. Barry was both an Airborne Jumpmaster and Instructor Pilot and served in two areas of combat including Vietnam. Chaplain Barry is an ordained Senior Chaplain with Chaplaincy Nevada serving as Director of Administration and the Advisory Board. He is the Team Leader with 10,000Kids (producer of Emmy nominee Trafficked-No-More); RECAP (Reclaiming Every City Around Peace) First Responder; Lead Chaplain for Red Rock Search & Rescue; Mayor's Faith Based Initiative on Human Trafficking Moderator; and is a METRO Volunteer. Barry is also a certified Maxwell Leadership Course Instructor.

Barry has 45 years of experience in the securities industry. For the last 22 years, Barry is serving as an Arbitrator for the Financial Industries Regulatory Authority.

Turning Challenges Into Opportunities

By Senior Chaplain Barry A. Mainardi

Our Faith will allow us to combat Satan's efforts. Sounds easy, doesn't it? Well, if it were easy, Satan would stop trying to delude us. Satan has many methods with which he will try to convince us that we are not loved or respected by God, our friends and acquaintances. His main target is our minds and thoughts as he attacks our self-esteem, as he reminds us of all our faults rather than the good we have done for others during our lives.

"We are pressed on every side by troubles, but we are not crushed. We are perplexed, but not driven to despair. We are hunted down, but never abandoned by God. We get knocked down, but we are not destroyed." (2 Corinthians 4:8-9)

Most of us dwell on our mistakes. The more mistakes we make, the more negative thoughts about who we are enter our minds. Negative thoughts such as, "…I should have done …", "… why did I do that …", "… I will never forgive myself …", "… I will never amount to anything …", "… I can't trust myself …" begin to dominate our thought process. Thoughts lead to actions and negative thoughts lead to negative actions; that are where Satan will try to take control. The results of his control will cause actions which will result in omitting God from our lives, lost jobs, dysfunctional families, unwanted or undesirable friends, reduced career opportunities and in severe cases, lost lives. All because Satan is trying to "take away" our self-esteem.

"Be alert and of sober mind. Your enemy the devil prowls around like a roaring lion looking for someone to devour. Resist him, stand firm in the faith, because you know the family of believers throughout the world is undergoing the same kind of sufferings" (1 Peter 5:8-9)

I am living proof that these attacks by Satan can affect one's life. There have been many occasions that I climbed that "secular success mountain" only to fall off that pinnacle because I still felt I had to prove myself ... to me. For many years, I experienced negative thoughts that controlled my life and the actions I took would always result in failure. Though, our Lord would always allow me to recover, each time it would take longer to climb from the hole I dug for myself. To make matters worse, my negative thoughts began to override my positive thought process and the need to isolate became my escape. What I did not realize was I not only remained in that hole mentally and emotionally, but each negative action would result in a deeper hole. Had I not asked the Lord for help, the consequences could have been catastrophic for me.

"The Lord is the One who redeems our lives from destruction" (Psalm 103:4)

Since we are discussing potential "why I can't ..." motives, I have several challenges in my life which, if not for my Faith, could have resulted in a "non-action" on my part. I am afflicted with a rare form of muscular dystrophy. During the last three years I had a triple bypass surgery and carotid artery surgery; and I am still recovering from a broken arm which occurred during one of my periodic falls (my mind makes commitments my body cannot keep). Even though I was surrounded by these emotional and physical challenges, I never gave up. I kept persevering because the Holy Spirit kept telling me that HE will always be there for me. All I had to do is "never quit". I am blessed because I am not a quitter though in the past not knowing when to walk away did hurt me on occasion. I finally discovered that there is a difference between being a quitter and knowing when to walk away.

"Faith is the confidence that what we hope for will actually happen; it gives us assurance about things we cannot see" (Hebrews 11:1)

All believers had a life-changing "Road to Damascus" experience and I am no different. My "Road-Experience" was life changing but unlike Paul, it took a while for me to wake up from the fall. Slowly I began to change my life beginning with what I call my "life envelope". Basically, I envision myself living inside an envelope and the edges of that envelope are occupied with responsible Faith-Based Believers and Christian Groups dedicated to serving our community, community leaders, mentors and individuals who want to make a difference in our community. No matter where I turn there is a positive influence in my life. I am also blessed because I am considered a leader in most organizations with whom I associate. All those I have selected to surround me are my "mentors" and I have received counsel from them on many occasions. Finally, notwithstanding the consequences passed down by God for violating His trust in me, I do not dare leave my envelope because I will be dishonoring all those who trust and respect me.

"Walk with the wise and become wise, for a companion of fools suffers harm" (Proverbs 13:20)

My son Tony was instrumental in my "transformation also. He and I were having a discussion and he was telling me that I was a great father to his sister and him. I do not take compliments well so I told him when I look in the mirror, I do not see the person he is describing. His response made a pronounced effect on me as he said, "Let me put this in a way in which you will understand. Are you telling me that God made a mistake?" I now look in a mirror in a different "Light".

My thought process has changed significantly because MY FAITH is telling me that Satan is and will continue to attempt to divert me; however, He will be there for me as long as I keep my faith. I now understand that making mistakes is part of the learning process … as long as we take responsibility for those mistakes and learn from them. As my faith grew, so did the memories of all the experiences in my life where our Lord granted me mercy and grace by saving my life or at least saving me from serious bodily harm.

There are many experiences, which could have tested my faith, but I used the events to help others and set an example on how God uses us for His Glory. I will only list a few and I pray these experiences open the eyes of our readers to increase your faith.

- Surviving an accident driving a car over a cliff (black ice) which put me in a hospital for a year

- Several life-changing experiences in combat

- Muscular Dystrophy

- Congestive Heart Failure

- Several major surgeries (one extremely critical and not originally diagnosed)

… and many more too numerous to articulate. Every situation where I thought I failed or missed an opportunity in my life turned out for the better for me. Every time Satan threw a barrier in my path, God has been there for me. Every step I have taken, He has guided me but I did not realize it until I opened my "faith-eyes" to see clearly. He has opened doors for me and given me discernment when my choices were "door #1" or "door #2".

> *"I know your deeds. See, I have placed before you an open door that no one can shut. I know that you have little strength, yet you have kept my word and have not denied my name"*
> *(Revelation 3:8)*

I also learned that we could always turn what seems to be a physical or emotional limitation into a tool to do God's work. While I was hospitalized for recent surgeries, and the heart surgery "confined me" for almost a month, I had opportunities to discuss my faith by being positive and helping doctors and nurses who visited my room. Nurses visited my room frequently to discuss "faith" and "hope" because I was living my Faith and not just "hoping".

Case Study … on me: When I first arrived at the VA Hospital in Los Angeles (open Heart surgery), a group of doctors visited my room. The head doctor (I could identify him because he was the only staff member without a pen or clip board) said to me, "Mr. Mainardi, we have a problem. Your records indicate that you have muscular dystrophy and have a tendency to fall. This surgery will require many hours of walking & physical therapy. Our concern is if you fall, you may seriously hurt yourself or even die. I waited for a few seconds and responded, "Doc, my Lord Jesus Christ told me to have this surgery so I could do his work. I am not concerned about the recovery portion of this process. What time is the surgery?" The doctor smiled and replied, "Will 6:30AM work for you … ", to which I responded, "I will be here". As the doctors left the room, I could hear comments like, "he is confident", "what faith he has", "I like his strength", and more.

I have many more testimonies, which demonstrate how I use whatever limitations or perceived negative emotional challenges as tools to help others. Attending classes in a wheelchair with post operational or "post break" pain is an inspiration to others. However, I must honestly say I "push myself" to encourage me as well as to encourage others. I discovered the more we quit, the easier it is to … quit. We are all different and we tolerate varying degrees of pain and suffering but we can at least try.

"So do not fear, for I am with you; do not be dismayed, for I am your God. I will strengthen you and help you; I will uphold you with my righteous right hand" (Isaiah 41:10)

We must understand that the devil is not going to afflict us, and neither is God. There are accidents, illnesses and other events that seem tragic that occur in our lives and these are opportunities for us to reach others. However, the devil will try to use our minds to create a "poor me" attitude so we do not continue to follow the path God has set for us. If the devil puts a road-block in our path, we must use his actions to our advantage which means for God's purpose. I visit the VA facility in Las Vegas frequently and always have an opportunity to encourage not only veterans but VA staff members also. Had I not had these limitations, I would not have the opportunity to serve Him to help other combat veterans. Recently I attended a VA medical facility to receive ongoing treatment for my broken arm. During the appointment, one of the staff began discussing a grieving issue that had been bothering him for several years. The staff member asked me what I thought. We discussed the grieving process at length and when I left, the staff member was appreciative of my comments and thanked me for my assistance.

Personally, the negative thoughts we all experience could have been disastrous for me because I am afflicted with Post Traumatic Stress Disorder (PTSD). However, they are minimized because of my faith and my understanding of how PTSD affects those who are afflicted. When they do appear, I remember my son Tony's question to me. In fact, negative thoughts actually simplify life for me. I feel the Holy Spirit speaks to me in my thoughts. Sometimes it is difficult for some of us to differentiate between the Holy Spirit speaking to us or the enemy speaking to us. In my case, it is somewhat simplified. If it is a negative thought, it must be coming from the "enemy". All other thoughts must be from the Holy Spirit.

> *"By their fruit you will recognize them. Do people pick grapes from thorn bushes, or figs from thistles? Likewise, every good tree bears good fruit, but a bad tree bears bad fruit. A good tree cannot bear bad fruit, and a bad tree cannot bear good fruit. Every tree that does not bear good fruit is cut down and thrown into the fire. Thus, by their fruit you will recognize them"* (Matthew 7:16-20)

Satan will always attempt to divert our attention from the mission on which our Lord sends us. The good news is we can use those negative deflections as tools to help others. But only Faith can allow us to see the path I just described. No matter what physical or emotional limitations we experience, we will succeed only because of our FAITH. He selected us because of our Faith. He foresaw our strengths and weaknesses and decided we were "right" for the job. Without Faith, we cannot defeat Satan, our enemy. We cannot traverse the path our Lord set for us without Him.

"For we know, brothers loved by God, that He has chosen you, because our gospel came to you not only in word, but also in power and in the Holy Spirit and with full conviction. You know what kind of men we proved to be among you for your sake. And you became imitators of us and of the Lord, for you received the word in much affliction, with the joy of the Holy Spirit"
(1 Thessalonians 1:4-6)

Finally, we must be prepared for the work for which He chooses us by living The Word and reading The Word. We must find scriptures that will assist us to do His work. Some of us, including me, are task and goal oriented and as such read with those purposes in mind. For example, I "search" for a few scriptures that support my strengths and help me combat my weaknesses. Sometimes "memory" does not work, so I recommend writing the scriptures on cards or using our "smart phones" and review them to make certain we are still on the path He set for us. Do not lean on our own understanding because Satan is waiting just around the corner to divert us.

"Trust in the Lord with all thine heart; and lean not unto thine own understanding. In all thy ways acknowledge him, and he shall direct thy paths" (Proverbs 3:5-6)

Senior Chaplain Bryan Ostaszewski

Reverend Bryan Ostaszewski, is an Ordained Nondenominational Christian Minister and Ordained Chaplain. He has been involved in religious-theology practices and studies for over 28 years and has additional education and experience with many different religions. He provides Chaplain services to many local major Hospitals, Hospice and Rehabilitation facilities in Southern Nevada. He is a Certified Pastoral trained Counselor providing: Marriage, Family, Spiritual, Grief and General Life Guidance. He is a Motivational Speaker, a Certified Christian Life Coach, a Consultant and Special Events Coordinator, and is also a Nevada State Licensed Wedding Officiant and Notary Public. Rev. Bryan is also a national certified and registered Suicide awareness and Intervention trainer for: YMHFA, SafeTalk and ASIST. He is also a first responder, disaster chaplain and works with the American Red cross and the Medical Reserve Corps. As a volunteer and has completed additional study in Criminology, Profiling and Forensic Science.

My Journey of Strength

By Senior Chaplain Bryan Ostaszewski

Faith is wisdom and strength that we find within ourselves, which the Lord has given to each of us, but also defines our calling. In our life we are placed on many journeys where we learn more about ourselves. We learn to accept our weaknesses and learn to love ourselves for who and what we are. We all need to accept ourselves, embrace our personalities and even our imperfections, knowing that although we are not where we need to be, we are making progress. Jesus died for us because we have weaknesses and imperfections, and we don't have to reject ourselves because of them. God wants us to love ourselves and enjoy how He's made us, just as we are!

"This is how God showed his love among us: He sent his one and only Son into the world that we might live through him. This is love: not that we loved God, but that he loved us and sent his Son as an atoning sacrifice for our sins. Friends, since God so loved us, we also ought to love one another." (1 John 4:9-11)

Our dear Lord places us on many journeys. Through these journeys we experience, personal growth, strength and wisdom. Regardless of the journey, we always seem to become better developed than we originally were. Our Lord created each of us with his own hands, a majestic masterpiece in his creation. He then continues to chisel away at us, "a little bit here and a little bit there" every day, continuing to improve the final result. I am certain proof that my life has been transformed through these journeys.

When I was 12 years old, my mother was diagnosed with stage 3 lung cancer. This was extremely devastating to my family, especially since she had two young children, myself and my sister and an adopted 18-month baby boy. My grandmother watched my sister and I, while my father continued to work his normal long shifts and then spent most of his time away from home and was at the hospital each day.

The terrible morning finally came when I knew my mom had to have surgery. The surgeon had to stop her heart and put her on a machine, while they removed two lower lobes of her left lung. The surgery lasted 16 hours, longer than usual. Because of this, the surgical team had difficulty getting my mother's heart to beat on its own. Technically, my mother was physically dead for 4 minutes, and this information had traveled to the nurses desk on the floor of my mother's room.

As we were waiting, hours felt like days. Finally, my grandmother called the hospital to try and find out my mother's current condition. Unfortunately, my grandmother was told that my mother had just expired. I can't begin to tell you the sadness and overwhelming pain my sister, my grandmother, and I felt. My whole world had come to a sudden stop. What was I going to do without my mother? After all, she was also one of my best friends.

However, unknown to us at that time, we were given the incorrect news. My grandmother was frantic, while attempting to get in contact with my father. Little did we all know, that my mother was doing fine. She had been moved to ICU and my father was sitting with her in recovery. My father had no idea that we had received the incorrect news. Finally, my grandmother contacted him and broke the news of my mothers passing. Needless to say, my father was livid. He corrected her and we all felt a major relief. After several weeks, my mother was discharged and came home. That was one of the most wonderful days I had ever experienced.

"But blessed are those who trust in the Lord and have made the Lord their hope and confidence. They are like trees planted along a riverbank, with roots that reach deep into the water. Such trees are not bothered by the heat or worried by long months of drought. Their leaves stay green, and they go right on producing delicious fruit. O Lord, you alone can heal me; you alone can save. My praises are for you alone." (Jeremiah 17:7-8, 14 NLT)

A few months went by, when one of our neighbors across the street from our home had a major catastrophe. The parents of my best friend were killed in a car accident. The funeral had come and gone, and the home was dark and cold. I remember one afternoon, I finally saw my friend come out of his house and just sat on his curb. His head was down and he looked so unhappy. I immediately remembered how I felt when I thought my mother had died; so empty and lonely. So, I decided to talk with him and explain what I had experienced. In no time at all, his tears and sadness began to turn into a little more hope, because someone took the time to reach out to him.

"Love God with all your heart, and love your neighbor as yourself"
(Matt. 22)

My mother continued gaining her strength, and the years continued to roll by, actually 15 in all. Then one spring in 1976 she came down with a very bad case of pneumonia. This was extremely worrisome due to her condition. She went back to her doctor for a CAT scan and found out that her cancer had returned, this time being Non-

Hodgkin's Lymphoma. It had spread throughout portions of her lymph nodes. Her Oncologist wanted to take immediate action with chemo therapy and radiation.

I remember taking her to one of her weekly infusion sessions. There were several individuals with some type of cancer, receiving their weekly treatments. Patients just sitting in chairs, back to front of each other, with just a few nurses coming and going. But, no one bothered to come and talk with any of them.

I had been sitting with my mother for hours. I asked one of the nurses if they had any chaplains or spiritual care staff that came to speak to any of the patients. I was told there were some resources, but, the patient would have to speak with his or her social worker and request a visit. I was overwhelmed with anger and disgust. I felt these individuals did not ask for this disease, and they certainly deserved better care. I asked where the Chaplains office was and went down to their department, only to find two individuals sitting and talking. I asked how often they go and visit patients. Their reply was every hour. I found that strange, as I had been sitting with my mother for hours, but no one came into that infusion department. I searched my soul with prayer, asking my God what could I do, to not only help my mother through this torturous journey, but, also the others as well.

Needless to say, I felt called to become a Minister. This was not far from the norm, as my uncle had been a Pastor in a church in Northern California, and he had asked me many times if I was ever going to give God's ministry a chance

"For I was hungry and you gave me food, I was thirsty and you gave me drink, I was a stranger and you welcomed me, I was naked and you clothed me, I was sick and you visited me, I was in prison and

you came to me. Then the righteous will answer him, saying, 'Lord, when did we see you hungry and feed you, or thirsty and give you drink? And when did we see you a stranger and welcome you, or naked and clothe you? And when did we see you sick or in prison and visit you?' And the King will answer them, 'Truly, I say to you, as you did it to one of the least of these my brothers, you did it to me"' (Matthew 25:35-40 ESV)

My mother's cancer, once again, was in remission and we enjoyed many more years together, enjoying the day to day of life until she began to have some major pain in her groin area. She found a major lump, so went to her doctor for another scan. Sure enough, her Non-Hodgkin's Lymphoma had returned.

Her Oncologist stated that she would have to go through chemo therapy again, but this time the treatment would have to be a little more aggressive. Her doctor created a special "chemo cocktail" known as the "Red Devil." This time, during her treatments, unlike her others, she began losing her hair, and I noticed my mother's mental outlook was slowly declining more than usual.

I would visit my mother every other day, due to my work schedule, and I had many of her neighbors check up on her for me. One afternoon, I received a call from one of her neighbors, very concerned about her heath and her eating habits. She was refusing to eat, and felt there was no further need for her to stay on this earth. I remember her Oncologist speaking with us about this normal mind-altering issue, especially with aggressive chemo therapy treatments, but, I could not believe that this would be happening to my mother. So I went to visit my mother. One of her neighbor friends was waiting for me, and warned me about her attitude. I did visit her and she must had lost at least 50 pounds. I couldn't believe what I was seeing, in such a very short time. I questioned my mother, and she stated that there was nothing to live for. She was on her chemo treatment number 2 of 7 sessions, and there was no way that she was going to get through this.

Again, I had remembered what her Oncologist explained to me, about the day I may have to use some reverse negative psychology. So, I left her room for a moment and told her neighbors located in the next room, that they may hear me say a few things they may disagree with. Then I went back into the room and sat with her. I again asked if she would eat something for me and she refused, and became very angry and belligerent. She stated she has nothing to live for, so why try. So I asked her, "am I not something good enough to stick around?" She just looked at me and said nothing. So I mustered up the strength and stated, "then if you feel there is nothing to live for, go ahead, just give up and die." That was the last straw! She became extremely angry at me, and told me to please leave.

I personally knew what I was doing but, I felt so devastated that I had spoken to my mother in that way. So, I did leave. However, within the next 24 hours, I received an update from one of the neighbors that my mother was beginning to eat again, and she did make it through the remaining chemo treatments, she felt would be impossible. A few months later, my mother asked me a question. She stated that she did not raise her son to speak to her in that way. I agreed, but responded, "That may be true, but, you also didn't raise your son to just quit when things were tough and give up, either." She just looked at me and stated, "We will talk about this later."

A few weeks later, I realized that I needed to be able to provide more than just comfort and support to patients. This led me to seek training to become a certified Pastoral Counselor. I also took Spiritual Leadership Classes, specifically for cancer patients, through the Cancer Treatment Centers Of America, Cancer Care Leadership Program.

"The Spirit of the Lord GOD is upon me; because the LORD hath anointed me to preach good tidings unto the meek; he hath sent me to bind up the brokenhearted, to proclaim liberty to the captives, and the opening of the prison to them that are bound." (Isaiah 61:1-2)

Many years have since gone by, and I have become more active in my community, volunteering many hours of my time with many organizations, continuing additional study, to be even more prepared for almost any issue that would come my way.

Unfortunately, at age 87, my mother's cancer has returned. This time the Non-Hodgkin's Lymphoma has come back, even more aggressive than ever. In fact, the cancer now has spread to most of her internal organs, including both lungs. Her Oncologist suggested that she make a final decision. My mother and I sat down for a serious discussion. She looked at me and asked "If she didn't fight my cancer this time, would you be angry with me?" I looked at her and stated "you have put up a great fight over the years, and you have every right to make up your mind. I would honor any decision you would make." After all, she is not only my mother, but, has always been my best friend.

Currently, she has hospice home care, is on constant oxygen, and still has her ability to walk around her one-bedroom apartment, though bobbing and weaving. Her independence is still one of her main desires and opportunities for now. Watching this has also brought me to yet another service in my line of efforts and callings to work with Hospice Care organizations in our community. I know that her time remaining on this earth is limited, but, she has taught me what strength and faith really is. She has given me a true insight of what providing services to others in the name of our Lord and Savior really means. I will always be grateful for what she has done for me, and how our Dear Lord has used me, his vessel, to serve others, in his name, honor and glory!

"Don't be troubled. You trust God, now trust in me. There are many rooms in my Father's home, and I am going to prepare a place for you. If this were not so, I would tell you plainly. When everything is ready, I will come and get you, so that you will always be with me where I am. And you know where I am going and how to get there."
(John 14:1-4 NLT)

Senior Chaplain Sally StJohn

Sally StJohn is an ordained and licensed minister in Nevada. She serves Chaplaincy NV as their Vice Chair, on their ethics committee and as their lead instructor in Clinical Pastoral Education. Author, talk show host, StJohn has over ten years' experience as the on-air success expert for many TV and radio networks. She earned her BA in psychology (1981-1985), MS in counseling from UNLV (1986-1990), and PhD in Psychological Counseling from LaSalle University, LA (1992-1996). She is a Licensed Alcohol and Drug Abuse Counselor (LADC) and Certified Rehabilitation Counselor (CRC). She's the director of UNLV's Career Connect, where she helps students with disabilities to find work they love. A sought-after speaker/trainer, StJohn lectures nationally and through social media on her publications, including: The Truth Reflex, The Instant Answer and The Vantage Point. Her passion is helping people reconnect with God. Visit Sally: ChaplainSallyStJohn@gmail.com sallystjohn.com, Facebook or LinkedIn.

Faith Waits

By Senior Chaplain Sally StJohn

I don't know how people do it … how they can believe in something they've never seen. I didn't. I wasn't made that way. I was the type that needed proof. For me to believe it was real, I had to see it, feel it, hear it, experience it … and that started way back when I was a kid. I wanted to believe … like my neighbor Mrs. Garrett believed. I just couldn't. Until December 14, 1991, when my heart stopped beating in the recovery room of a Los Angeles hospital. After that, I didn't need faith. There was only one thing I needed, and I finally 'got it.'

Faith, like everything else, is a very personal, private, deal. It doesn't matter what everybody else says "Faith is" … what matters is what you feel in your heart faith is, and whether you'd bet your life on it, because one day you will. To people who already have faith, hearing stories about faith can make them feel all warm and wonderful … but, what if you don't have faith? Or, what if you're on the fence? Or what if you've placed the idea of faith in the same box as religion … and religion in the same box as God, and you decided, like I had, that there was something not quite right about religion? What then? Do you throw it all out? Do you risk living your life without faith? Do you risk dying without it? Do you stay undecided?

Hebrews 11:1 says "Faith is confidence in what we hope for and assurance about what we do not see." That made absolutely no sense to me - then. And that, in a nut shell, was my problem. I, like a lot of left-brain, logical thinkers, had to understand something to believe it.

If it didn't make perfect sense, or if I didn't read it in a (text) book, it probably wasn't true. There were so many things about that scripture and the bible that didn't make sense to me when I was young. God himself could have shown me proof that He was real and I might have still kept my arms tightly crossed … and missed it.

Not that the whole 'God-Thing' (as I used to mockingly call it) didn't intrigue me. It did, in an annoying sort of incessant way. Like a tiny splinter in my finger, I couldn't leave it alone. I couldn't take my mind off it, but I couldn't quite grab it either. In elementary school, I would ride my bike … miles … to St. Mary's on Wednesday nights to sing in the choir … with a bunch of grown-ups to music that was horrible. (Why would a kid do this?) I went to Sunday school (on Saturday) … for years and didn't really get anything out of it, except that my friends went, so it was kinda fun – and I finished my sacraments, which was important, I guess. Because I believed then, that if I didn't do that, I wasn't going to heaven … which made even less sense to me. Then I went back to church on Sundays with the Garrett's. I remember kneeling, sitting, standing, kneeling, sitting, standing . . . looking around at people's faces . . . and hoping, one day, I would feel, understand, or "get" – even a piece of what Mrs. Garrett got . . . but nothing.

Mrs. Garrett was my best friend's mom. She lived down the street. She'd take me to church because my mom worked. She'd make breakfast, banana curl my hair, and make sure I was dressed just so. She treated me like one of her own – and she had several. Six. Five girls, and Christopher, and she'd pack us all in the station wagon and away we'd go. One Sunday after church, I asked Mrs. Garrett how she knew for certain that God was real? She said, "Oh, SallyAnn, you gotta have faith… Just talk to Him, like I do… in prayer."

I didn't really understand what she meant, but I could tell she believed what she was saying, so I believed her. Since Mrs. Garrett had already demonstrated her prowess in installing banana curls and making chocolate cake, I decided that I was going to give this a try. So I started with the standard prayers Catholics say. I recited the Hail Mary. I recited the Our Father. They didn't work. So, I did what Catholics do, I said them again … over and over … on my knees, but they still didn't work. But I didn't give up. I lit a candle … two. I went to confession. Still, nothing. Then I felt bad that I left something out of confession so I had to go back and confess about confession. Still, nothing. But still, not giving up.

I went to the library. I spent hours, hunkered down reading anything I could get my hands on about praying, and God, angels, the universe. I looked through books, and Bibles and pictures, hoping something, anything, could explain the vastness of this God-Thing. I tried just opening up the bible and reading the first thing I saw, thinking God might have a message just for me. I tried reading just the parts in red letters (those were my favorites!) I thought I understood those parts the most, but then I'd read them again, and it was like I was reading them for the first time! Sometimes, the only thing that would make my nightmares go away was taking the Bible off my bookshelf. I would get under the covers read the red letter parts with my flashlight and it would put me right to sleep. But still, no big "Aha!"

One night, my family was clearing the dinner table. We were still reeling over the news of my 17 year-old cousin's tragic death. He was killed in a drive-by shooting in New Jersey. "Thank God Aunt Rose's faith is strong," my mother said. I stopped for a moment, 'Really Mom??, I said to myself. 'Faith is enough to get her through that?' I also thought to myself, how odd it was for her to say anything about faith since she never went to church, and, with the exception of grace over dinner, I don't think I ever saw her pray. You see, my parents were equally yoked in their distaste for organized religion. The only time they went to church was when someone was getting married, baptized or buried. They pretty much threw the Baby out with the holy water.

Like I was saying. Faith is personal. You come to it or run from it for your own reasons. My parents had theirs ... and theirs shaped mine. My mom's brother, Uncle Louie, was a kind man. Everyone who met him liked him. My mom considered him a role model. She looked up to him for support, guidance and protection. He was her big brother ... in a big city ... in a tough time. New York, 1942. To this day, my mother shows me the picture of her brother, and she still gets choked up. He was a very handsome man. Sharp dresser. He had these big, blue, eyes. And he was talented. He could play the violin . . . "effortlessly ... like he'd been playing forever." He was engaged to be married when he was drafted. He didn't have to go, because my grandmother had polio, but he went, and died in St Lo France, in 1944. He was 19. My mother was heartbroken. She blamed God and I don't think she ever forgave Him.

My father's story, slightly different. He spent his first three (3) years in Italy, being raised by his mother's sister, 'the sister' ... in a convent. His mother had to leave him there because he was sick and she had the opportunity to come to America and set up a new life for the whole family. Knowing she would return for him, and that this would be best for the whole family, she painstakingly left her baby boy behind. Fast-forward three years being raised in a convent / orphanage ... even though you have a mommy ... she's not there. The damage was done. He equated God with religion with abandonment. Yet he was protected and surrounded.

70

As my father grew, he, and others, realized he had a gift. My father was an exceptionally strong athlete and swimmer and was scouted by the Olympics in a public pool in New York City as a teen. He could dive and not splash. He had a strong, flawless stroke and kick. He could hold his breath and swim underwater for several minutes. Excited, he ran home and told his mother about the Olympic offer. "Whata dis Olympics? Forgettaboutit!" Less than a year later, he lied about his age, and volunteered for the draft at age 17. In 1945, my father, now a U.S. Marine, fought in Iwo Jima. He credits his survival to God and had expressed his gratitude for what he knows were God-given gifts – one of which was his ability to swim.

After my niece's baptism, I was talking to my father's cousin from the convent, Father Frank. Father Frank, who swore he would remain a missionary and live a life of poverty forever, had now moved to America and was living in Mastic Beach on Long Island. Because I was the only one who had completed all the sacraments, I got to be the "God-mother" even though I was just 11 … so I was already on Father Frank's good side. I figured I'd ask him the question –the question I ask everyone. "Father Frank, how do you know God is Real? He stopped laughing and gave me the same answer in his thick Italian accent, "You gotta hava faith." I probably should have stopped there, but I didn't. "I don't understand, Father Frank. How do you believe in something you can't see?" You don aska that question. You jus gotta believe." Again, I probably should have just kept quiet. But I really wanted to know, and this was my big chance. So I had to ask him the BIG QUESTION. The splinter question that was stuck in my head, that if he could just answer this one question, I might be able to take that leap of faith. "Father Frank, how is it that Jesus, the Holy Spirit, God are the same, but different? . . . that confuses me." He stopped. He turned to my father and said, "Tony? What is it with this one? She no suppose aska this question. She eating the tree of knowing.   You just need to have faith."

Later that day, Father Frank and my mother had a conversation. He told my mother she was going to go to hell because she ate meat on Friday. She told him, "Father Frank, I believe in God. I believe in Jesus. I love my husband. I'm faithful to him. I don't lie. And you're telling me because I eat meat on Friday, I'm going to hell? I got news for you, I'm going to have a lot of company!" Our family was not invited back to his church or its functions.

That whole thing left a sour taste in my mouth ... for Catholicism and religion in general. I asked my mother if it was OK that I checked out my friend's church ... the Episcopalian church. She said, "if that's where you want to go, go ... as long as you go." So I left the Catholic church and ended up at St. Marks. I liked it there. They were warmer, with all the pancakes, square dances, small groups, but I still wasn't feeling what I felt like I should be feeling and I knew it. I started wondering if I would ever feel it. Then I thought, what if there's nothing to feel? What if this whole God-thing isn't even real? What if Jesus was the last of the made-up stories parents tell you, like The Tooth Fairy, Santa Claus, and the Easter Bunny ... and that you find out about the God-thing when you're 21 or when you die or something?

Or something. On December 14, 1991, in the recovery room of a Los Angeles hospital, where the good doctors were supposed to be, my heart stopped beating. I died. I learned quickly that I did not need faith. I had proof. He spoke to me ... and I recognized His voice ... from forever. Jesus! What I learned, as I lifted up out of my body and started zooming at warp-speed down the whitest brightest 'tunnel' of what I now know to be the light of our Lord and Savior Jesus Christ was that He truly is the Prince of Peace and that He was with me all along ... from the beginning of time ... and that he will never leave me ... ever. He showed me grace, love, nothing like we have here on this planet. And of course, I had to ask the question: How do I know you're real? But finally, He had the answer. "Remember that question you asked Father Frank? … The answer is ICE. Like ice, I AM … then it all clicked. Ice – water – steam; Body – Mind – Spirit; Jesus - Holy Spirit – God. Then it all clicked.

He is God in the physical dimension "Why didn't Father Frank explain it like that?" I asked. "Because he couldn't." He is the Truth, He is the way, and the life. He is love. He is the light. He is inside every cell of your body. He is very much alive … but He is not religion … He is relationship, and He'd been trying to have a relationship with me … forever. I just wasn't ready to receive Him, so He waited. He's trying to have a relationship with you too. He's waiting … for you to invite him in.

Senior Chaplain Shelea Griffith

I was blessed of the Lord with the Holy Spirit at the young age of ten in the city of Rochester, New York. By 12, I was singing in the choir, and a member of the Jr. Usher Board. Later, I was appointed the Sunday School Teacher for the Catechism Class, Junior Class and later the Sunday School Secretary.

Later, I became a Deaconess, President of the Pastor's Aide Committee, Editor of the Church Newsletter, Chairman for the Welcome Committee, Event Planner, Photographer, Director of the Youth Department, the After-School Program, and Counselor for troubled teens.

I am an ordained Senior Chaplain through Messages of Faith Ministry, a Radio Co-Host through Blog Talk Radio, the Executive Coordinator through "Men In Search of Change", and a Mentor with Hope For Prisoners.

I consider working for the Master as the core of my Spiritual Life.

AMAZING

By Senior Chaplain Shelea A. Griffith

Praise God from Whom All Blessings Flow! Without FAITH, we know we cannot please God. Unless we completely believe and trust God, FAITH will not show up on the scene. Our FAITH is an amazing powerful tool when we truly need it.

Thus, my story begins. My name is Shelea and I was born to Irene and Samuel Lucas, on December 23 in Rochester, New York. They both were working in the same Factory in New York City. As they both left work to go home; they were standing at the corner now waiting for the traffic light to turn green to proceed toward their destination.

This was the time and the moment of love when their eyes glanced at each other for the first time; and bells begin to ring all around them. He gave her such a captivating look. She smiled and turned away. It was as though he had seen a perfect angel. The entire area where they both were standing lit up like the Bethlehem Star.

He asked her for a name. She giggled and replied, "my name is Irene". He cleared his throat, and in a very deep romantic voice replied, "What a pleasure it is to meet you, Madame", and my name is Sir Samuel. At that moment, their hearts began to beat to the tune of a different drum. Love was truly in the air. After they switched telephone numbers; the rest was history.

As more time evolved, the relationship became very serious. Mom felt like a marriage proposal was in the air. She decided to ask him if there was a problem with their relationship? He finally broke down to let her know what the situation was. He told her he loved her very much; but he was married. His wife was an alcoholic for many years, and he was very unhappy. After waiting 5 years for a change, he left the country to find happiness elsewhere.

Mom recently found out that she was pregnant, and together they danced, and cried and shouted for joy. This would be his first offspring. He so badly wanted to have children. He was the happiest man in the world, and he would do anything if they could get married. They both agreed it was praying time on a daily basis, morning, lunch time and evening. They decided to have Faith in God, trust and believe, and know that everything was going to be all right, in God's own time.

Because they were not married at the time, and I was ready to come into the world; a huge decision had to be made. My mom lived in a one-room studio house. Her Landlord told her that no children could live there; it was only for adult residence. So, they decided it would be best for me to live with her best friend, Martha and Frank Clark, whom she had known for over 15 years.

(DRUM ROLE) It was December 23, Thursday evening at 4:01 PM when God decided that it was my time to enter this awesome world. When I was born, I weighed 3 lbs. and 5 ounces and was small enough to be held in one hand. My lungs were not fully developed and my heart rate was up and down. I had to breathe with a ventilator. I was fed through a tube every two hours. The nurses checked on my condition every ten minutes. I became the favorite of every nurse. My parents stayed in a hospital room every night, to be there for me as they prayed for me while exhibiting the FAITH to believe and leave me into the hands of Almighty God in His own time.

The Doctor wanted me to weigh over 5 pounds before giving me a clean Bill of Health. With much prayer, my lungs and breathing patterns became above average, and my heart rate became stable. After a strong report from a team of Doctors and a million prayers from everywhere and everybody, and weighing a total of 6 pounds, I was released to leave the hospital and live a some-what normal life. And so, life began for me. I was three months old when I left the hospital in the protective arms of a loving mother; Martha Clark and her husband Frank Clark. Martha was a licensed Foster Mother and Frank was a Judge in the Courtroom.

Growing up in a big house full of laughter from 12 kids and loving parents, I was truly blessed. At age 10, I began to pray, read the Bible my parents bought me, and tell stories from the Bible to anyone who would listen to me. My Dad always taught me to do my best to become successful, and I should always have FAITH and believe God for a Miracle even when life seems unbearable. I began to be a risk-taker and was never afraid to try new things.

It was January 10th, a day that came with a few scattered pieces of a puzzle. I was in the family room playing with my sisters and brothers, and mom called me to come into the living room. She came out of the living room to meet me half way to changed my shoes and brush my hair as she gently kissed me on my forehead. She informed me I had a visitor in the living room that wanted to speak to me.

As I entered the living room, I was introduced to a very beautiful woman wearing pretty clothes and jewelry; and then my Mom suddenly left the room. So, I just sat on the couch wondering who could this unknown lady be and listen to her speak., She reached into a big bag and pulled out the prettiest doll I had ever seen. She was almost as tall as me. I smiled and said, "Is this for me?" She said, "Well of course it is just for you". "I said thank you very much, I will take good care of her". Mom came back in and told me to say good night.

I finally got up the nerve to ask Mom, who the lady was that gave me such a beautiful gift? She said, "She is a good friend of mine." A month later, the unknown Lady came back for another visit with me and more gifts. As time went by, the visits became more regular and closer together. However, I began to look forward to her visit. I really loved it when she gave me a hug and a kiss. There seemed to be a different feeling about it. It just made me feel happy. In the meantime, the love birds were doing exceptionally well. They were continually trusting God, and having the FAITH to believe that everything was going to be alright. In the next ten days, Sir Samuel received a Certified Letter stating that his wife had passed away. He flew home to Barbados, West Indies to funeralize and legally finalize the conception of that marriage.

After returning to the USA, they set a wedding date and were happily married on November 10th. As months of Jubilee went by, now came the time to put the complete plan of action in place. The unknown Lady came for a special visit. My Mom was in the living room for quite a while speaking with her. Without my knowledge, the "Day of Pure Reckoning" came into my life.

Mom came out to take me into my bedroom to freshen me up a little bit. I noticed one tear dropped from her eye. She kissed me on both cheeks and gave me a big hug that followed with the words, "The unknown Lady is your Mother and she is here to take you home with her. But you don't have to go with her if you don't want to go now". I immediately decided I was not going to go with her and this must have been a mistake. The moment of time had finally come. My Mom and Dad both introduced the unfamiliar Lady to me as my "Mother". Then she took off running across the floor toward me, with big tear drops flowing down her face. "I love you so very much" she said. She gave me the tightest hug and longest kiss I had ever had and I loved every moment of it. In walked a pretty little girl smiling from ear to ear. I had to look at her twice; because I thought

I was looking in a mirror. She looked exactly like me. The Lady I now knew as my Mother said, "This is your baby sister, Her name is Mary". I said, "Hello". She smiled and said, "I am home by myself with nobody to play with. Will you come home and play with me"?

My eyes began to fill up with water as teardrops ran down my face. I hugged her and said, "Sure I will come and play with you!" I have lots of toys and I will share them with you. She smiled at me and said, "Ok. Our Daddy is home waiting for you."

We all hugged each other and everyone began to cry tears of joy. My other sisters and brothers also hugged and kissed me on my check with tears of joy for me. They were informed earlier regarding the event. My bags were already packed along with all my toys. We each said a prayer and after more hugs and kisses from my parents, I said, " How can I have two Moms and two Dads?" My Dad said, "It is a true Miracle from God." Continue to have FAITH and nothing but good things will come to you. Always trust God and He will never leave you or forsake you in any kind of situation.

Meeting my Father for the first time was super exciting. He kissed me, picked me up, threw me in the air, and twirled me around several times with more kisses than I could remember. My Mother cooked a special dinner. We all sat around the table with nothing but laugher that filled the air. My Dad put on some music and we all danced for a while. My sister and I finally had the chance to go outside and play with each other. This was my first Miracle. And my life again was wonderful, exciting and full of love and laughter. Before you knew it, the year was about to end.

It was finally December 22, and my birthday was just hours away. I couldn't wait to go to sleep, so when I wake up, it would be my special day. I will be 11 years old. My birthday party starts at 4:00 PM. All my special friends will be coming to my house as well as my other sisters and brothers, and Mom and Dad whom I love with all my heart. Yes, I really went to sleep with a big smile on my face. Tomorrow will be the best and happiest day of my entire life.

My Mom woke my sister and me up screaming. I was very puzzled because it was still nighttime. It was very dark and there was smoke everywhere. She told us to quickly get up and hold hands with her to follow her into the kitchen. The smoke was darker in the kitchen, so it was very hard to see. We yelled for our Dad; but we could not find him.

She opened two windows in the kitchen and said, "Do exactly what I say. Jump out the window now or you will die." My baby sister jumped out first. I followed as I felt the heat of the fire upon me. My Mom did not have time to jump; the fire was on the hem of her bathrobe. She fell out the window and landed near where our car was parked in the back yard of our three-story apartment building.

We all were crying because we felt that Dad had died in the fire, since none of us could find him in the dark or hear his voice. My Mom, sister and I were all rushed to the nearest hospital emergency department. While in the ambulance, we would say, "Lord give us the FAITH to Believe that everything is going to be alright."

My sister had a broken leg. My spine was crushed at the end of my back and my Mom had 3rd degree burns all over her body, a broken leg and both arms broken. While Mom was in the operation room, we sent up a prayer for her body to be healed. My sister and I had beds in the same room. We still were concerned about our Dad. We had not seen him or heard from him. We lifted his name before God.

Miraculously, Dad came in to our hospital room with his wheelchair to see if we were all right; after leaving Mom's hospital room. Dad was so glad to see us; he just cried and began to thank God for all our Miracles. He began to tell his side of the story. We were in the back of our apartment; but he was in the front standing on the ledge. As he was about to jump, he was told to wait. The Fire Marshall placed a ladder near the ledge for him to climb down to safety. He could not stop crying as he was thinking; we were all lost in the fire.

While spending my 11th Birthday in the hospital, we realized we lost everything in the fire; but we had each other and that was a true Blessing! Even though we all were in different hospital rooms, except my Dad, who was staying with a friend; we ALL were in constant prayer and had the FAITH to believe a Miracle. We ALL were alive and had each other to comfort and love.

Our church found us a beautiful place to live. The Red Cross provided us with clothes, food, and furniture. Three months later, we ALL were healed, able to walk and leave the hospital. God truly showed up and showed out as he blessed us to begin our new life. My two families came together every month to pray, fellowship and give God all the Praise!

Oh! By the way, both my parents surprised me with a bigger birthday party three months later. All by the Grace of God. I saw the tragedy as a MIRACLE. Having two Moms and two Dads is truly a Miracle from God. I felt so happy and blessed to have so much love from so many people. We all agreed, without FAITH, we couldn't please God!

OUR FAITH IS AN AMAZING POWERFUL TOOL. It will always be there when you really need it... Just Believe!

Senior Chaplain Pamela R. Poston

Pamela R. Poston is happily married and serves in ministry with her husband, Overseer and Senior Pastor Walter L. Poston of Highways and Hedges Outreach Ministries (www.Highway4JC.com). Both are Chicago, IL natives.

March 2006, Pamela was license and ordained into ministry as an Evangelist. December 2010, she was ordained as a Chaplain, then to Sr. Chaplain with Messages of Faith Ministry in Las Vegas, NV. July 2011, Sr. Chaplain Poston was again elevated and ordained as Pastor through LFC Apostolic Community Network of Kingdom Churches & Ministries of Chicago, IL. 2015, she became the author of Answers to Relational Healing 101.

She serves in County and State adult and youth prisons and jails. Pastor Poston has lead countless souls to Jesus Christ through testimony, teaching and preaching of His saving, healing and delivering power!

According to John 8:36, "*I'm FREE INDEED!*"

Blessings Through Blind Faith

By Senior Chaplain Pamela R. Poston

Dictionary.com describes *Blind Faith* as: "*Belief without true understanding or perception.*"

"*The LORD had said to Abram, 'Go from your country, your people and your father's household to the land I will show you.'*" (Genesis 12:1 NIV)

Genesis 12:1 is very familiar to my husband and me. The same God that spoke to Abram, said similar words to us. He wanted us to go into the jails and prisons to minister to individuals seeking hope. Our *blind faith* moved us from Chicago, Illinois to Las Vegas, Nevada, in the peak of the 2009 recession, which left us homeless.

We were newlyweds, celebrating one wonderful year of marriage. Why would God tell us to resign from our full-time employment with benefits, to relocate to a city of financial unease at such a time as this? We asked ourselves, "*Why should we resign from good jobs, during the peak of a recession, when things were going so well for us?*" In 2009, Las Vegas ranked the second highest unemployment rate in the nation. Were we being setup by satan? Did we mishear God's voice?

We read scriptures such as: "*⁵Trust in the Lord with all thine heart; and lean not unto thine own understanding. ⁶In all thy ways acknowledge him, and he shall direct thy paths.*" (Proverbs 3:5-6) "*So then faith cometh by hearing, and hearing by the word of God.*" (Romans 10:17) "*Now faith is the substance of things hoped for, the evidence of things not seen."* (Hebrews 11:1) *"But without faith it is impossible to please him: for he that cometh to God must believe that he is, and that he is a rewarder of them that diligently seek him."* (Hebrews 11:6) (all scriptures - KJV)

Oh, how individuals are so quick to quote such idioms as: *"If I believe it, I'll receive it.", "It's my time and it's my turn.", "Touch your neighbor and tell them, 'It's yours!'", "Where's your faith?"* and so on. We sing songs about faith. We quote scriptures by memory about faith. Our faith scriptures are plastered on walls, computers and mirrors. We even have bumper stickers and tee-shirts to prove we have faith. We even teach and/or preach about our faith. But when it's time to live and walk in obedience of faith, many of us rationalize why we can't do what needs to be done, and/or we allow other chattering voices to diminish those beliefs.

Our obedience came through God giving these relocation instructions to my husband during a vacation in Las Vegas, May 2009. Added obedience came through my detailed testimony released in my first book, <u>Answers to Relational Healing 101 - Including Testimony and Teachings: How Pain Can Become Your Purpose</u>. In this book, my testimony journey describes how God's faithfulness, deliverance, and healing power brought me through crime, emptiness, fear, homosexuality, and rebellion. It also includes, 78 hard to talk about relational healing questions and answers.

Questions, questions and more questions came from our loved ones and mirrored those we had ourselves. When we received this commandment from the Lord, we prayed, consecrated and fasted ten weeks for confirmation. Afterwards, God still told us to, *"Go."* After a while, we shared these instructions from God with our family and friends. Some family members were against our decision, which affected our relationships for years. This was due to my parents' health conditions.

After loading limited belongings in our vehicles, we headed to Ingalls Memorial Hospital located in Harvey, Illinois, where my mother was fighting cancerous cells caused by Multiple Myeloma. I was so emotionally and physically ill that day, that I regurgitated in her hospital room. And to my dismay, she was living out her last days.

Our planned two-day trip from Chicago to Las Vegas turned into a five-day journey. A few of our travel tests and trials included encountering a snowstorm, our vehicle overheated, tire problems, fearful mountain and cliffs peaking 10,000 feet above sea level (approximately the height of seven Empire State Buildings in New York City).

Five days later, we arrived in Las Vegas tired, hungry and homeless. We checked into a hotel off of the famous Las Vegas Strip and settled in for a few days. Prior to our departure, we had a prayer meeting with a group of intercessors. At that meeting, the Lord financially blessed us through a sister in Christ. She said, *"The Lord told me to give you all $1000 for your journey to Nevada."* Hallelujah!

As our money started to run out, we began living out of our SUV in a parking lot of one of the major Hotel and Casinos on the Las Vegas Strip. We bathed in their restrooms and visited food banks and churches for meals. Neither of us knew homelessness on this level of hot days and very cold nights. But through it all, God protected us and remained faithful to us.

Later, we were blessed to receive loans from a few loved ones back home. We had enough to rent another hotel room week to week. While there, we called help-wanted ads, temporary employment agencies, and prisons, to become volunteers.

Days later, we received mail at our PO Box from the Nevada Department of Corrections, stating our prison volunteer applications were denied due to lack of information. Fear gripped me, because I had two past felony charges in Las Vegas. I was distraught with the thought of a complete denial because of my past. We immediately went on a three-day consecration of fasting and praying for God to work out this situation. We resubmitted our applications. In these three-days God prevailed!

We were approved to serve in several Nevada State Penal Institutions. We started a Bible Study class at High Desert State Prison, a maximum-security men's facility that retain over 4,000 men. Later, we obtained approval at the City of Las Vegas Detention Center where I had been incarcerated. Then we were approved to serve at the Women's Prisons where I would have served up to 30 years for two felony charges; *attempted murder and battery with a deadly weapon*, as well as *being on the run for 17 months*. But God!

We continue to witness God's miraculous saving and deliverance power in so many lives at these jails and prisons. Inmates had shared, *"Hearing your testimony of God's mercy, gives me hope!"*

During our job searches, I contacted a temporary agency where I was employed in the past. They finally scheduled an interview, after my persistence. Upon arrival, dressed in a suit with my business folder; I was escorted to meet with an Employment Specialist. After minutes into my interview, I was asked to go on an interview at one of Las Vegas largest social service agencies. After registering and computer tests, I had to hurry to the interview.

As I traveled the busy road of South Eastern Avenue on that sunny afternoon to my interview, I had to read a brochure about eight divisions at this company at each stop light. Upon arrival, I encountered a line of individuals waiting to ask questions. After stating my request, I finally met with my interviewer. She was a very pleasant and professional lady. She asked a list of interview questions and then reviewed my resume. Afterwards, she asked: *"Why did you recently move here from Illinois?"* I replied, *"My husband and I moved here on a mission and assignment from God to volunteer in prisons and jails."* She seemed surprised by my answer; but the interview continued. Moments later, she replied with words such as: "*After reviewing your resume, you do not have all of the qualifications and skills required for this position, but you do have the heart I need of helping people. Part of our mission here is to help people with helping themselves. After hearing why you and your husband relocated here; I am convinced I have found the right person.*" She previously interviewed several other candidates. After passing a urine analysis, she hired me on the spot, as her Executive Assistant. At the end of our meeting, I asked for her business card because I wasn't sure of who exactly I'd be working for or her title. To my amazement, she was the President and CEO of the company! This reminds me how Proverbs 18:16 (ISV) says: "*A person's gift opens doors for him, bringing him access to important people.*"

After several months of homelessness and now with full-time employment, we were able to move into our own apartment. Even though, we had to sleep on the floor. Later, we were blessed by a sweet young lady we met to lend us a mattress to sleep on. We were so grateful to finally have permanent residence.

However, my husband was still underemployed. He worked short-term temporary assignments while seeking permanent full-time employment. These were true testing times. As bills continued to come in, he volunteered on weekends during the holiday season to distribute food and gifts to low income families with me, at my place of employment. After a while, his volunteer service and hard work paid off.

Three months after our departure from Chicago, on Sunday, Valentine's Day, I received a telephone call from my family. "*If you want to see our mother alive again, you must come back to Chicago immediately!*" I called my boss to share that I needed to go home right away. She approved and I flew back to Chicago the next morning.

I arrived midmorning to a partly cloudy, snowy and frigid day and called my parents' home to let my family know my plane had landed safely. My god-mother picked me up from the airport and we headed straight there. By the time we arrived, my sister met me at the door with a very sad message. *"Right after you called, we believe mom heard your plane landed safely, she took her last breath!"* I fainted. Through the help of the Fire Station, located right across the street from my parents' home, I regained my composure and went into the living room where my mom was lying in a hospice bed. Words cannot describe my loss. Later the same year, we returned to Chicago to bury my god-mother. The next year, we returned to bury my father.

My parents were praying individuals, who prayed and fasted many days until I received my healing and freedom from bondages of my sin. We studied, traveled and ministered together, spreading the gospel of Jesus Christ. I was very close to both my parents. My mom and god-mother were my best friends. They taught me how to be a godly woman. They mentored me after the death of my first husband. They were my greatest supporters in marrying my current husband.

Traveling to Chicago each time was a financial hardship on us. But again, God stretched our money and made a way. This resulted in sleeping on our borrowed mattress for additional months thereafter, but God was still faithful.

After arriving back in Las Vegas, my boss told a manager she could hire my husband to work in her department. I was so happy; I could have jumped on the desk to celebrate! However, that happiness was short lived when I found out the hours weren't conducive with our after-work volunteer hours for prison ministry. When the meeting with that manager concluded, I immediately went into a new found prayer closet (the restroom across from my office). I locked the door and petitioned the *Throne of Grace.* I prayed a prayer such as, *"Lord I am humble and grateful for this full-time employment opportunity for my husband, but Lord the second shift hours will not work. Father, I do not know how you are going to fix this, but I have faith you will. In Jesus name I pray. Amen!"*

When I left that restroom (my new prayer closet), I went back into my office and continued to work. I shared nothing about this situation or prayers with anyone. I didn't even call my husband. I held onto the faith I just released and waited on God. A short time thereafter, my boss hastily came into my office to share some wonderful news. She said something like; *"Pamela, guess what? Another position just became available in our Homeless Services Department as a Case Manager, and it is the same hours as yours! So, now you and your husband can do your after-work prison volunteering!"* Then shared such as*: "But that's not all, it's paying thousands of dollars more than the other job!"* When I called my husband, we rejoiced and praised our awesome God!

It is almost seven years later and my husband is still employed in serving the southern Nevada homeless population. During this tenure, he was chosen to exclusively work with the homeless veterans' population, because of his military services.

After a year as the President's Executive Assistant, another position became available in the agencies' Youth Department. I always desired to work with youth, but lacked the academic requirements. The Lord allowed me to find favor with our president and the director. As a result, that position was offered to me. With much hard work, I became the lead, then the supervisor, which lead to a promotion as manager of two Youth Employment and Training Programs. Both of these programs specialized in serving Southern Nevada's homeless youth. I supervised a staff of 16 individuals, located at various locations: Our main campus, seven Clark County High Schools and two rural offices. Now, this is what faith in God can do! James 2:17 (NIV) says: *"In the same way, faith by itself, if it is not accompanied by action, is dead."*

As the Lord blessed Abraham and Sarah with Isaac, He then asked for their promised son to be a sacrifice. Employed now in my dream career job, I was asked to have faith in God and sacrifice my employment. Therefore, I submitted an eight-week resignation letter and resigned from my job.

Over the years, I received prophecy after prophecy to journal because I would become an author. My husband supported my decision of employment resignation and I sacrificed my dream job (my Isaac). Out of that sacrifice, my promised child was conceived (my book), <u>Answers to Relational Healing 101 - Including Testimony and Teachings: How Pain Can Become Your Purpose</u>.

A year after my book was completed, I was hired back at my former place of employment. I have humbly submitted to my current manager (a staff person I hired under my supervision). I am trusting God every step of the way with anticipation of His continuous awesomeness! *"Your beginnings will seem humble, so prosperous will your future be."* (Job 8:7 NIV)

God blessed us through *Blind Faith* with wonderful employment to serve Nevada's homeless population (from which we came), with compassion and appreciation.

"For as the body without the spirit is dead, so faith without works is dead also." (James 2:26 KJV)

Senior Chaplain Walter L. Poston

Walter L. Poston received Jesus Christ as his Lord and Savior in Chicago, Illinois in 1978. He was later baptized August of 1978 at Ayers Chapel Church of God in Christ (C.O.G.I.C.) in Kirchgoens, West Germany while serving his country in the U.S. Armed Forces.

While in Germany, Overseer Poston participated in various Bible studies. He received the baptism of the Holy Ghost on December 31, 1979.

After returning to the United States, Poston joined St. John COGIC in June of 1980. He also joined and served in ministry with Reeves Temple and Abounding Life COGIC churches until God called him to pastor House of Refuge Church of God in Christ in 1999.

Overseer Poston continued to pastor in Illinois until God commanded he and his wife (Pastor Pamela) to relocate to Las Vegas, NV where they serve as Outreach Pastors.

I Was Only a Child

By Senior Chaplain Walter Poston

There are many people who have gone through various kinds of abuse. Some have experienced physical, verbal, psychological, or even sexual abuse. Anyone who experiences any or all of these different types of abuse can develop deep-rooted pain and bitterness. Abuse can traumatize the life of the individual, who is now going through or has gone through mistreatment. Abuse can change the course of their lives; reshape the way they view themselves, authority, family and the world. It could severely damage the victims' self-worth, and steal years from their lives, oftentimes, incarcerating their soul and deceiving them to believe their future is grim.

As a young child, I was forced to carry a heavy burden that only God would be able to destroy. I was only a child. Why me?

The answer has become the passion within my purpose; the reason I decided to write about my life. I hope my testimony will encourage and help those whose spirit and soul are broken due to sexual exploitation. Jesus said:

> *"For God so loved the world, that he gave his only begotten Son,*
> *that whosoever believeth in him should not perish,*
> *but have everlasting life."* (John 3:16 KJV)

It all began one day, when I was playing in my parents' three-bedroom apartment. I looked out the window, the sun was shining, the clouds were white, and the sky was blue. I was enjoying the beautiful day as I ran throughout the apartment playing with my toys. Suddenly, I heard my cousin calling my name, *"Walter, come here,*" she called out to me. I ran into the bed room to inquire what she wanted. She was lying on the bed nude. She commanded me to pull down my pants, and get on top of her. I became confused, as we had sexual intercourse, while another relative watched. I didn't understand what was happening to my young innocent body.

The sun continued to shine, but my soul and spirit entered a place of darkness and bondage. The works of flesh were manifested, and the law of sin had an open door in my members. The Apostle Paul wrote; "*Now the works of the flesh are manifest, which are these; adultery, fornication, uncleanness, lasciviousness*" (Galatians 5:19). He also wrote; "*I see another law in my members, warring against the law of my mind, and bringing me into captivity to the law of sin which is in my members.*" (Romans 7:23). Shame, confusion, fear, and discouragement became my companions. The shame was so painful, that I didn't share the experience with my parents. I feared it would destroy the unity of our family. Oftentimes when sin and shame of abuse are confessed to parents, they help or seek assistance to provide counseling to young victims, which provide tools for recovery.

The demons entered my soul, possessed my spirit, and used my body for evil works. These ungodly spirits controlled the very core value of my being. This molestation expediently introduced a 5 to 8-year-old child to adulthood. I was not mature enough to comprehend the ramifications of what had transpired. I began to have dreams and nightmares of death, and perverted intercourse, which brought on wet dreams and succubus spirits.

I became academically challenged throughout my school years. I struggled with who I had become. As a teenager, I began to abuse alcohol and illegal drugs to self-medicate the deep-rooted pain I experienced daily. I remember a group of my friends would gather together, listen to hard rock music, abuse alcohol and drugs, and view pornographic magazines. During this season of my journey the devil tempted me with living a homosexual life style, but I rejected the temptation and refused to give in to seducing spirits. Nevertheless, sexual thoughts continued to work mightily in my mind, keeping me in captivity to sin.

During my high school years, I devoted a lot of my time developing athletic and musical skills. I joined the Hirsch High School marching band, where I learned how to read music and play the bass guitar and bass tuba. I also learned how to play basketball and baseball. I tried out for the high school baseball team, but wasn't successful. The coach informed me that I would be placed on the team as a penchant runner. I became discouraged, and didn't return to practice with the team. Nevertheless, I continued performing with the high school band. My musical skills with the bass guitar and tuba developed very fast, because the band instructor demanded perfection. Therefore, I put in long hours of practice; which taught me that if I desire to be good at anything, I must devote quality time to it.

I later joined a community band in the Chicagoland area where I lived. The band traveled and performed at different nightclubs throughout the city. I remember some of the musicians abused drugs during rehearsal, and before performances at nightclubs. I thought the band would give me a sense of belonging that would heal me, but it took my soul deeper into a dark cave.

I met a beautiful, fair skinned young lady in my last year of high school; her name was Pamela. We became good friends and began to date, but I didn't understand what was required for a healthy relationship. Pamela was the first female I allowed to get anywhere near my heart. Due to trust issues, I wouldn't open the door of communication. She was a strong, intelligent young teenager. I was a young broken-hearted male who was looking for someone to love him and become his Savior. I didn't know Jesus during this time, so I depended on people for help. My inability to communicate my true feelings kept my emotions incarcerated.

This became a problem in our relationship, because Pamela loved to communicate, but I didn't. She tried numerous times to get me to open and communicate to her. After a while, she became very frustrated with my non-communication, and ended the relationship. I felt discouraged and rejected because I didn't have a date for my high school senior prom. Even though I didn't attend the prom, I managed to graduate from high school, and signed up in the United States Army in June of 1977.

Approximately a week after I graduated from high school, my mother was transporting me to the airport for a flight to South Carolina. She was proud that I completed high school, but heartbroken that I enlisted in the Army. I was nervous because this was my first flight, and I didn't know where this decision would lead me. Nevertheless, determination pushed me into my purpose. I communicated to my Aunt Vickie that I was going to get out of Chicago. I arrived in South Carolina along with other men from various States. We were instructed to get into an eighteen-wheeler cattle truck that transported us to Fort Jackson for eight weeks of training. I will never forget what happened to all of us young trainees once that cattle truck arrived at its destination. A tall sergeant, in a green military uniform, shouted at us trainees; *"You have two minutes to get out of the truck."* We all gathered our personal items, and departed the truck very quickly. Basic training was very difficult, but it taught us how to be men. The training officers were hard on us, because they were training us to be skilled soldiers. God would later teach me how to be a good solider in His army. I completed and graduated from basic training. I also completed an additional eight weeks of training to become a military cook.

The military deported me in November of 1977, after I had completed all my trainings. I was assigned to the 564 Military Police Department in the small town of Butzback, Germany. There were approximately three African-American soldiers assigned to this unit. We were persecuted and discriminated against, because of the color of our skin. Nevertheless, we continued to serve our country with honor, and didn't allow hatred and bitterness to fill our hearts. We were trained to fight against the enemies of our Nation. God, in His wisdom, used the hatred that was aimed to discourage me, to lead me unto salvation.

During this time of persecution, I met an African-American soldier named Willis, who was from the State of Kentucky. Willis and I became very good friends until I became a Christian. During our time off on weekends, we would travel to different parts of Germany, enjoying the beautiful country side. Other times, we visited different nightclubs, strip clubs, and prostitute houses. Doing ungodly things, thinking we were having a good time.

I remember many days of feeling lonely, empty, and hopeless, but I continued to walk down this path of darkness. My sinful flesh was being fulfilled, but my soul was empty and void of God's Spirit. The Apostle Paul wrote; *"Know ye not, that to whom ye yield yourselves servants to obey, his servants ye are to whom you obey; whether of sin unto death, or of obedience unto righteousness?"* (Romans 6:16 KJV). The demons possessed my soul, as I enjoyed the pleasures of sin for a season. I was a slave to the sinful desires of my flesh. The Apostle Paul also penned; *"For the wages of sin is death; but the gift of God is eternal life through Jesus Christ our Lord."* (Romans 6:23 KJV).

In the year of 1978, things began to change in my life through several events. The desire to read the Bible started weighing on my mind. This was very perplexing to me, because my friend and I were still enjoying the pleasures of sin. The desires to read God's word consistently invaded my thoughts. I didn't understand what was happening to my mind, because at that time I was spiritually blind, separated from God, and possessed with demon spirits. God had mercy on my soul. His Spirit was drawing me to Christ for salvation. Jesus said,

"No man can come to me, except the Father which hath sent me draw him: and I will raise him up at the last day." (John 6.44 KJV)

In June of 1978, I returned home from Germany on a thirty-day military leave. I still didn't understand what was taking place in my thoughts; confused about the void feelings I felt. I thought, *"Maybe I'm lonely"*, so I decided to reconnect with my high school sweet heart, Pamela; only to discover she had married one month prior to me returning home. Then I thought; *"Maybe, if I played my bass guitar again, I would feel better."* I later found out one of my siblings sold my bass amplifier. This was very discouraging, but God had removed everything that would hinder His plan of salvation for my life. Even though I didn't marry my high school sweet heart; in

2008 I married Pamela Taylor, who loves me the way I need to be loved.

One day, as I was walking to the corner of 8127 South Dante Avenue, I saw one of my friends, LaCarlton Williams, witnessing to a man about Jesus. I stood near to hear the conversation they were having. My friend was witnessing about committing sexual sins. The more I heard him witness about Jesus, the more my soul desired to inquire about this Jesus. Something within me discerned that this was He for whom I had been searching; Jesus the Son of God! After my friend finished communicating with the man, I began to ask him many questions about Christ and life. LaCarlton couldn't answer some of the questions, because he had just received Christ a month prior to me returning home. Therefore, he took me over to his cousin Cleophus' apartment.

His cousin Cleophus was an Evangelist, filled with the Holy Ghost, and full of the Word of God. I asked them many questions about Christ and life. He answered all my questions with scriptures. They both labored with me for hours, ministering to the brokenness of my soul. The demons that possessed my soul for many years were now being tormented by the Gospel of Jesus Christ, (they didn't want to loosen the stronghold of the evil influences they had in my life). Evangelist Cleophus asked me if I wanted to be saved; I replied, *"Yes"*. He then instructed me to meet him at church the next day.

On Sunday, June 25, 1978, I arrived at the church. I sat in the back row of the sanctuary, and listened to the gospel message his Pastor preached. I enjoyed the fellowship experience, but couldn't rest until I received Jesus Christ. After church service ended, Evangelist Cleophus and I went into a small dark green colored room. He laid his hands on me and prayed the prayer for salvation. He prayed with the power and authority of the Holy Spirit. While he was praying, I felt the evil spirits leaving my body, and the burden of sin being lifted from my soul. This was an awesome feeling; my soul was finally freed from the bondage of sin and evil. Jesus said; *"If the Son therefore shall make you free, ye shall be free indeed."* (John 8:36 KJV)

I left the church, with joy of the Lord in my heart. I informed my friend, LaCarlton, about my conversion. He was very excited that I received Jesus Christ into my heart. We began to fellowship together until my 30-day leave ended. I expressed my concerns about not having a church to attend once I returned to Germany. He prophesied to me, stating; *"God will lead you to a church."* When I returned to Germany, God fulfilled those words. He led me to a church, where I joined and began fellowshipping with other believers until my tour was completed. I attended weekly bible studies and worship services. My faith grew in the Lord, as the Holy Spirit revealed God's word in me. *"So, then faith cometh by hearing, and hearing by the word of God."* (Romans 10:17 KJV)

These are just a few of the testimonies I included. There are many more I will share in my upcoming book. I praise God for the things He has done, to God be the glory. I can truly say, *"Faith Is... a journey"*. God can take you from a dark place, and transform your life into His glorious light. The Lord Jesus took what the devil meant for evil, and turned it to good. Now, *"The pain of my past is the passion of my purpose. He hath sent me to bring healing to the broken hearted."*

"Therefore, my beloved brethren, be ye stedfast, unmovable, always abounding in the work of the Lord, forasmuch as ye know that your labour is not in vain in the Lord."
(1 Corinthians 15:58 KJV).
Be healed in Jesus name!!!

Chaplain Amber

Chaplain Amber resides in Las Vegas, Nevada. She has been a Chaplain with Messages of Faith Ministry since 2014.

Touched by God

By Chaplain Amber

I restlessly wait for sleep to embrace me. There is an eerie and uneasy feeling all around. I open my eyes and scan the room. Everything seems normal, yet I am still not at ease. I take a deep breath and close my eyes. Suddenly, it intensifies into a feeling of dark wickedness. Something is wrong.

As panic sets in I am reluctant to open my eyes, yet I muster the courage and intensely scan the room again. Petrified, I see darkness swarming all around me. It is pure evil. Frozen, engulfed by a fear of literally dying, I slam my eyes shut. As I pray to God to help me, it instantly went away. I let out a sigh of relief that it was over, yet still feeling unsafe and confused of what "that" was.

Suddenly, I feel an internal energy so intense it pulls at the core of my body literally arching my back slightly. This startles me for a second, but I am not fearful. Then, a beautiful burst of intense energy of love embraces and entangles me from head to toe. I feel as if my soul is awakened. I am calm and relaxed, as if I am wrapped in a blanket of lovingness, forgiveness, goodness and protection. I was heart heavy when the powerful energy suddenly left me just as intensely as when it came; what an amazing experience I can only best describe as being touched by God.

Several years before my "touched by God experience", my best friend and I were living together and we were constantly pondering the meaning of life. Both in our early twenties, we were fascinated by the whole subject. Any and all types of religions, spirituality, magical practices, etc. you name it, we studied it. As often as we could, we were in the bookstore reading anything we could get our hands on pertaining to the subject. Sitting on the floor, surrounded by books, soaking up as much information our sponge brains could soak in.

We debated and asked a lot of questions. Was there a God and an afterlife as well? Or was there just blackness almost like being asleep, never waking up and life is just "over". We had mixed emotions regarding the latter. Eventually, our mutual consensuses was it probably was unhealthy for us to worry about that too much because after all, if it is just "nothing" when we die, we wouldn't know or worry anyway because, well, we are dead. But on the other hand, that did not seem satisfying as we felt it in the core of our bodies there was "more" to it. So, we made a pact by promising each other if I died first, then I would prove to her there is a God (therefore an afterlife) if I was able to. She agreed to do the same. I just didn't realize it would only be a few years later that she would follow through with her promise. The night when I was embraced with the intense energy of love was the night she was killed in a car accident. Once I found out she had died, it all made sense why I was touched by God. She wanted to reassure me and to feel His love.

Just as I was so certain at one time that this life here on earth was "it", now I am certain there is more. I was shown there is a God and he is a loving God. The love I have for Him seems minuscule compared to how much he loves us, but to be closer to God is to love Him in return. By always trusting and having faith in God we are loving Him. God created us in His image and we are ALL God's children. The closer we are to Him, the more we can *receive* kindness, patience, love and empathy. To live through Him by *giving* kindness, patience, love and empathy results in living a fulfilled life serving Him.

I was shown evil and darkness. Love is more powerful than evil. It is essential not to allow negativity to consume us. Allow forgiveness towards ourselves and others, no matter what we are faced with. The darkness comes in many forms, such as fear, anger, insecurities, judgment, guilt, hate and despair. Even if we are suffering, we have to keep faith in God, to keep close to Him. Even though when you're suffering it definitely seems easier said than done sometimes. Over the years, since she died, I have struggled with this. Even after my very compelling experience feeling His love, sometimes I would lose faith and drift further away from Him when I felt riddled with guilt or despair. I questioned God, why her and not me? She was and is the friendliest person I have ever met.

She was just driving down the freeway going home one night and someone entered the wrong way onto the freeway. She was traveling West in the left travel lane and the other driver was traveling East in the same lane. She was hit head on and killed instantly.

I was especially angry at God once I found out more details of the accident because of the fact she was driving in the fast lane. I used to tell her all the time that driving in the fast lane was dangerous. The fast lane is for passing, so pass the slower car and get back over. She said she just felt more comfortable driving in that lane. If she would have listened to me and drove in the slow lane then the other car would have just drove right past her. Over the years I would particularly digress just for that reason and move further away from God and let the darkness consume me and ask Him, why did you not make her listen to me just that one time? Since then I've realized we all have free will to drive in any lane we want and it is not God's fault. Still, I wish she had remembered the one thing I had told her so many times before.

One night I was driving on a two-lane highway and I was pondering a question to God. Why did she not see the car coming towards her? If there was any distance at all then it seems like she would have seen the lights and moved over. You don't see lights on the freeway anyway, you see tail-lights. Strange, I thought. Well, just as I was thinking that I proceeded to pass a slower car in front of me. I saw bright lights far away. I had a long stretch of road, so was ready to hit the gas to pass and something inside of me screamed, no! I got back over behind the car I was ready to pass and a second later I saw the car that I thought was far away instantly beside me. Turns out it had one headlight out, so the perception seemed further away but in reality was very close. I pulled over to the side of the road, terrified, and felt the, "Oh God I almost was killed moment" and instantly realized why she might have not seen the car coming towards her. God had answered my question...again.

Faith is...keeping close to God. Becoming a chaplain has given me the opportunity to do just that. I have encountered many times in my life where I was struggling to keep him close. I know now He has always has been close to me. It is me that drifts away because of the darkness.

"It is the LORD who goes before you. He will be with you;

He will not leave you or forsake you. Do not fear or be dismayed"

(Deuteronomy 31:8).

Even today, writing this story is very emotional, yet very healing for me. I had to dig out the newspaper clipping of the accident to confirm some details, which I haven't looked at since it happened twelve years ago. I don't blame God anymore for what happened. I trust and love Him, no matter what. For whatever other reason I am here in Las Vegas I know I am here to serve Him any way I am able. Giving Glory to God is special, as special as being one of His children and what a beautiful gift back to Him by having an opportunity to share what my belief Faith Is...

Chaplain Karen R. Atlantic

Karen R. Atlantic, MS, BS is currently employed as a Licensing Worker for Clark County Department of Family Services whose passion is serving as part of a team to ensure the ongoing safety of children who are placed in the Child Welfare Foster Care System. Karen earned a Master's of Science Degree in Psychology and Community Counseling and a Bachelor's of Science Degree in Psychology, Sociology and Business Administration from Troy State University, Alabama.

October 21, 1976 Karen received Jesus Christ as her personal Lord and Savior. On October 09, 1991, Karen accepted the call of God and received her Ordination as an Evangelist. Karen has a heart for the things of God and serving people. Karen has traveled to several countries on Missions Trips that include: Peru, Honduras, Mexico, Amsterdam, Bermuda, Prague, Holland and several cities in Germany. The great commission is being fulfilled in her life in the USA. Karen will continue to go to other countries sharing the Gospel of Jesus Christ, but her heart is where God has planted her, at home, in the United States…at least for now.

Not In A Box

By Chaplain Karen R. Atlantic

Recently, I realized that I do not have any "dreams" for my future. Yes, I am a believer, a thither, a laborer in the up building of God's people and Kingdom here on Earth, sharing the "Good News" with people who do not know Jesus, serving and being a witness. Serving, Church attendance, spending time with the Lord, reading and studying my Bible: shouldn't these actions and commitments be enough of a dream for me? Should I want or desire more from God? A better question to ask myself is; do I think I deserve more? Sometimes, God uses people to nudge us, or we may experience an "inner something." I recognize this "inner something" as the Holy Spirit. The Holy Spirit has a way of nudging me from the inside. He reminds me that God knows the plans He has for me. Plans to prosper me and not to harm me, plans to give me hope and a future. "Lord, why don't I have any dreams?"

> *"For I know the plans I have for you" declares the Lord, "plans to prosper you and not to harm you, plans to give you hope and a future." Jeremiah 29:11 New International Version (NIV)*

I pondered these things in my heart and in my mind. Have I lost faith? I thought about washing machines. If I purchased a washing machine from Sears, would I call JC Penny's for a repair? NO! I would contact the manufacturer of the product. I began to examine myself as Paul encourages us to do.

> *"Examine and test and evaluate your own selves to see whether*

you are holding to your faith and
showing the proper fruits of it.
Test and prove yourselves [not
Christ]. Do you not yourselves
realize and know [thoroughly by
an ever-increasing experience]
that Jesus Christ is in you—
unless you are [counterfeits]
disapproved on trial and
rejected?" 2 Corinthians 13:5
Amplified Bible Classic Edition
(AMPC)

I was nudged even further. "And in all your getting, get understanding." That meant I needed to define words. Wikipedia Faith (disambiguation): "Faith, the confidence or trust in something or somebody despite the absence of proof." The Cambridge Dictionary defines trust as: "to have confidence in something, or believe in someone; to hope and expect that something is true." I Googled "Confidence:" "the feeling or belief that one can rely on someone or something; firm trust." Merriam Wester defines hope as: "archaic: trust, reliance; desire accompanied by expectation of or belief in fulfillment; also: expectation of fulfillment or success; someone or something on which hopes are centered; something hoped for." This led me to Hebrews 11:1 "Now faith is the substance of things hoped for; the evidence of things not seen."

I had no clue where the Holy Spirit was leading me, but I was going to follow! I became hard pressed to know why I did not have a dream. After giving myself a check-up from the neck up and everywhere in between, I thought I was holding to my faith and showing proper fruits, but something wasn't quite right. I asked God, my manufacturer; my Maker: "Lord, have I tied your hands or have I put you in a box?" I thought maybe I was doing something or there is something I should be doing and because of this, that perhaps God couldn't show me my dream. I wasn't really sure what "putting God in a box or tying His hands really meant.

I have heard these "sayings" numerous times from other believers, teachers of the Word and even preachers. Who else could I ask? Who else would know the answer to my heartfelt question? I want to know why I do not have a dream that is so big that it is destined to fail unless God is all over it, in it and through it! I want to have a God sized dream. God's Word is truth and light. People are people and we do people things - but not GOD. GOD is not like man (people) that He would ever tell a lie. The cry of my heart became, "I trust you Lord."

> *"God is not human, that he should lie, not a human being, that he should change his mind. Does he speak and then not act? Does he promise and not fulfill?" Numbers 23:19 New International Version (NIV)*

> *"Trust in the LORD with all your heart, and lean not on your own understanding; in all your ways submit to Him, and He will make your paths straight." Proverbs 3: 5-6 New International Version*

Oh my Father! My LORD! My Daddy GOD! My loving and caring patient Father, responded to this child in this way..."Notice the sky...the very heavens that you cannot look beyond. The stars, the moon, the atmosphere...I set in motion; separated and called into existence." As I began to look at the night sky, in seer admiration of the handiwork of GOD, I lost myself in thought. God did all that I see and beyond by His word. "Let there be..."

> *And God said, "Let there be light," and there was light. God saw that the light was good, and he separated the light from the darkness. God called the light*

*"day," and the darkness he
called "night." And there was
evening, and there was
morning—the first day. Genesis
1: 3-5 New International Version*

God, who is the creator of me, He knows me, how I think, act and do life. He recaptured my attention in such a way that is unmistakably a God move…"Do you think the universe can contain me?" aloud, I replied "No". He then said…"Why would you think you would or could ever place Me in a box or tie the hand that created the heavens and the earth and all above and below? It is you my child that is in a box. It is not my will for your life that you are in a box!" I inquired further…"how am I in a box?" He spoke-"It is your mind. Your mind is a box that limits your faith. It is not My limitless ability."

*Do not conform to the pattern of
this world, but be transformed by
the renewing of your mind. Then
you will be able to test and
approve what God's will is—his
good, pleasing and perfect will.
Romans 12:2 New International
Version (NIV)*

As I meditated on all the things that were told to me about me, I prayed that God would transform my mind according to His word, not how I think, rather how He thinks. I began have glimpses of understanding into how unknowingly, I had not opened myself to allow God to place a dream within me because I was in a box.

*What we have received is not the
spirit of the world, but the Spirit
who is from God, so that we may
understand what God has freely
given us. This is what we speak,
not in words taught us by human
wisdom but in words taught by*

*the Spirit, explaining spiritual
realities with Spirit-taught
words. The person without the
Spirit does not accept the things
that come from the Spirit of God
but considers them foolishness,
and cannot understand them
because they are discerned only
through the Spirit. 1
Corinthians 2: 12-14 New
International Version*

Do I dare step outside the box leaving the familiar to face in my own thinking that may appear to be wisdom but in truth is foolishness? Or am I able to utterly destroy the box? "Father I do not know what to do…"

*"We demolish arguments and
every pretension that sets itself
up against the knowledge of God,
and we take captive every
thought to make it obedient to
Christ." 2 Corinthians 10:5 New
International Version*

The warmth of God's love surrounded me as I trembled, and cried. I understood what I needed to do. In understanding what I needed to do, came a fear I had never experienced before. It was clothed in uncertainty. I had no doubt, hesitation or indecision about God or what He had shown me. I lacked confidence in my willingness or ability and unworthiness to conquer. I was nudged once again. "Greater is He that is in you than he that is in the world…you are more than a conqueror"

*"For the Spirit that God gave us
does not make us timid, but gives
us power, love and self-*

discipline." 2 Timothy 1:7 Good
News Translation (GNT)

"You, dear children, are from
God and have overcome them,
because the one who is in you is
greater than the one who is in the
world." 1 John 4:4 New
International Version (NIV)

"Yet in all these things we are
more than conquerors through
Him who loved us." Romans
8:37 New King James Version
(NKJV)

I arose from the floor to which I laid down on my face, prostrate before the LORD. I wiped the hot stream of tears from my face, with clenched fists, I declared in a loud voice: "You have no authority here, (pointing to my head), or here, (hand covering my heart). My stance became that of a warrior, my feet planted firmly into the carpet. You are a liar and a defeated foe. I will not adopt the thoughts you are attempting to plant in my mind nor will I fortify them by accepting them as my own. I pulled down every vain imagination that exalted itself against the knowledge of God, bringing every thought captive, under the obedience of Christ!"

I knew in that very moment my mind had been changed. The box was gone, utterly destroyed. How do I know? I know, that I know, that I know! It took me a few days to formulate the words to express what has happened to me. There are no limits in my thought life and there doesn't have to be! What is my evidence? I have a God sized dream that God planted inside me. My life has begun to change in many ways, ways that I would have never imagined possible! Being able to think in terms of God's limited-less ability through me and in me. I never knew that Faith could look like this. "Faith is the substance of things hoped for, the evidence of things not seen". My dream is beyond anything I would have thought or asked for myself.

I now have the mindset and faith to know that it's a God dream and He alone will accomplish the dream in me and through me. I have a favorable, confident expectation! My faith has given substance to my dream! The plans that God has for me are true. They will not harm me and I am not afraid. Every experience in my life has led me to this place; receiving and the ability to accept my God dream. My dream is growing. I am like a woman pregnant with a child. Would you like a glimpse of my God-sized dream? Please accept and understand that all I have is a glimpse, so this is all I am able to share with you now. My dream is unfolding every day, seeing dying men, women, children, hurt people, empty people, people trying to escape their lives by existing in alternate states, the beat down, misused, the abused, being saved, and...healed by my shadow.

More and more believers in the Lord, crowds of men and women, were constantly being added to their number, to such an extent that they even carried their sick out into the streets and put them on cots and sleeping pads, so that when Peter came by at least his shadow might fall on one of them [with healing power]. And the people from the towns in the vicinity of Jerusalem were coming together, bringing the sick and those who were tormented by unclean spirits, and they were all being healed.
Acts 5:14-16 Amplified Bible (AMP)

Not in a foreign country, land, or even in a third world country, but right here, in my community, right where I live. I am your next door neighbor whose heart breaks for the things that breaks the heart of God. He loves you so very much that he provided us with this opportunity to spend these moments together...just for you. Have faith to get out of your box to discover...your God-sized dream!

Chaplain Sara A. Bonaparte

Sara A Bonaparte is an Ordained Las Vegas Chaplain, Mental Health Professional, Personal and Business Career Coach for over 15 years who grew up in Las Vegas Nevada. Sara gained a unique insight into people through what she calls her life "internships" not just professionally but personally and uses those experiences to help others grow and serve. Presently, in her personal life she is raising 6 wonderful children, happily married to a wonderful man, that as her partner in life helps her now to pursue her calling and get the message of Gods love out to individuals that are lost and help them to find the connection, relationship and love of God.

Soldier Up

By Sara A Bonaparte

"Is there a chance?"
"There is a *50/50 chance* of the baby surviving, but it may have a
failure to thrive, possible brain damage and may also be blind"

I came into this world way ahead of earthly schedule at 28 weeks,
weighing only 2 pounds, 2 ounces. All my mother heard was,
"...there is a chance..." She prayed, along with my father and family,
to God to let me live and be healthy. My mother told God in her
prayer that HE could do whatever he wanted with me, just let me
live. "Soldier Up".

I am not my battles, I am not a victim and I am not the duties and
internships I have been given. They were and still are merely the
boot camp of life, simply the training I would require in the future of
God's plan to assist the people I am called as a Chaplain to light the
way for. As a Chaplain, I use the gifts of discernment and experience
to see the good, the gifts, and the strengths in other people in order to
discern where those gifts might be used. In this way I am able to
help, as a soldier in Christ, to build them up.

One may recognize the many battles I have been through: teen
parenthood, domestic violence, chronic illness, illness of a child,
building a home and divorce. I have been trained in many
internships: caregiver, single mother, wife, sister, daughter, chaplain,
hotel general manager, mental health provider and youth counselor.

I am a soldier of Christ, who has lived through many battles with

God-given grace, strengthening my faith by giving it all over to God, learning from each experience and in learning, establishing a routine of self-care. In caring for my armor, I am taking care of and nurturing my faith through prayer, the word and honest self-reflection.

My faith in God has gotten me through each battle. Make no mistake, I have been dealt many blows that have left physical and emotional scars, but I am healed through my faith. When a soldier of Christ is knocked to their knees, the battle has just begun, but through God's grace you will stand and you will succeed. I know I did.

Consistent practice is required to overcome any adversity simply through faith and growth in the relationship with God. Many say it is not "fair" what they have gone through, but that was simply training: A boot camp for those who have been called to serve, through taking action daily, hourly, minute or even by every second. Whenever required to block the attacks of the world, authority is obtained and established to speak, serve, and empathize.

 Through each battle, "Soldier Up" are the very words I hear in my heart and head when knocked to my knees in battle, at my weakest point, when I have given all I have to give that is in my human ability. It is then and only then that God lifts me up through his strength and grace, and pushes me onward. For it is not through my might, but His.

When I found myself in an apartment alone at 17 with a newborn daughter, "Soldier up". After the birth of my newborn son who died and was brought back, released out of the hospital and over the next year died five or more times and be brought back every time, to have the blessing of a beautiful, healthy 16 year old young man now, made each battle worth it. "Soldier up"

When my cousin and uncle disappeared while hiking and I was the caregiver for my grandmother and grandfather and had to support them and my young family through that time, to go through ten years of wonder of what happened to them; then have their remains found and have to go through the pain all over again, having questions never answered or new questions never dreamed of arising. "Soldier up"

When I found myself, after years of abuse, a divorced single mom of five with sole custody and no job. "Soldier up"
To learn that my calling was to become a Chaplain, a minister, and my first season was in hospice and then visiting and offering communion to those in the rural nursing homes that had been forgotten by their families as well as time itself. "Soldier Up"

As the matriarch of a "mixed" ethnicity family, I having experienced cruel racism by individuals and those in authority so terrible that I began to doubt humanity, only to be reminded, by the gratitude and love of my husband, children and those I serve, how wonderful people are." Soldier Up".

Life is a boot camp. The longer it takes one to arrive at God's calling and accept the calling as a soldier of Christ, the greater responsibility to share with others. My battle gear is my "armor"; it is my faith.
I must grow my armor like David did: I cannot copy what others have done. How can one copy a minister if one were not called to be a minister? It may not be the season to be a minister. David went up against Goliath, a giant, and a giant problem for David. Everyone gave advice or laughed at him; even a king, a successful man by all accounts, tried to give David his armor, but it was too big, and not at all what was needed by David for his giant. I have learned that many will seek to give you advice or try to push their "armor", their faith, on you. However, like David, you must trust in God to give you the tools to overcome the "giants" and grow. Make no mistake, David did grow to have the armor and faith of a king, but first he used a mere rock and slingshot to let God direct his course and remove the obstacle.

Many will, and have tried, with good intention, to lend me their armor or advise on the way they grew their faith during their seasons and battles of life, but like David found, it did not "fit" right, for it is not mine. As I have walked, run, and lived in faith, I must stop and care for, repair and strengthen my armor and the tools God has given me. I must practice through constant prayer to communicate with God to grow my faith, as well as provide spiritual care to those in need, for if I do nothing when times are calm I will not be prepared when attacked.

Winning is not what the world views as "winning"; winning as a soldier of Christ is coming through each battle with your faith, hope, and joy intact. Those are in one's head and heart. After each battle or attack I must check my faith, my armor, for damage, so I can repair it. *Faith is,* growing and caring for my armor, practicing, and preparing for battle, with only what God has given me. Moses went before a Pharaoh with a stick and David before a giant with nothing but a slingshot and rock. The size of your faith or number of your tools or gifts is irrelevant. Showing up with nothing more than a mustard seed of faith and letting God show through you is all that matter; it is just another example of how out of little grows much. Your growth with each battle is key.

Ephesians 6:11-20, from which I first drew inspiration for overcoming and pushing through each battle, and implementing action as a demonstration of my faith, I learned to acknowledge weakness, repair and grow my faith in my walk with Christ, and ultimately through a strengthened relationship with God, discovered and will spend my God-given lifetime pursuing my calling and purpose.

Ephesians 6:11-20 English Standard Version (ESV)
"11 Put on the whole armor of God, that you may be able to stand against the schemes of the devil. 12 For we do not wrestle against flesh and blood, but against the rulers, against the authorities, against the cosmic powers over this present darkness, against the spiritual forces of evil in the heavenly places.

13 Therefore take up the whole armor of God, that you may be able to withstand in the evil day, and having done all, to stand firm. 14 Stand therefore, having fastened on the belt of truth, and having put on the breastplate of righteousness, 15 and, as shoes for your feet, having put on the readiness given by the gospel of peace. 16 In all circumstances take up the shield of faith, with which you can extinguish all the flaming darts of the evil one; 17 and take the helmet of salvation, and the sword of the Spirit, which is the word of God, 18 praying at all times in the Spirit, with all prayer and supplication. To that end keep alert with all perseverance, making supplication for all the saints, 19 and also for me, that words may be given to me in opening my mouth boldly to proclaim the mystery of the gospel, 20 for which I am an ambassador in chains, that I may declare it boldly, as I ought to speak."

The Helmet of Salvation; I must consistently check my mind, to ensure it is focused on God's purpose and God's calling for my path and to seek it, acknowledging the miracles, gifts and simple blessings in life. If I am concerning myself about worldly matters, reflecting on matters that might cause strife, I have then damage somewhere on my helmet I know I must repair and then *shine* it, through prayer and scripture daily so there can be no further attack. The Breastplate of Righteousness; I *hammer* out the dents from the attacks of the world of lies, false accusations and reminders of my past, for the breastplate protects my heart and if not hammered out, all those attacks will reach my heart and cause me to forget that I am loved and forgiven by Christ. I reflect on the loves of my life, whatever they may be: children, art, music, family, my husband, and alone time in God's presence, as those are blessings and part of my purpose.

The Belt of Truth must be *tightened* daily; it is what keeps the heart and mind connected and secure. Should it slip or grow loose, I find myself being attacked and weakened with each blow, so tightening it grows more difficult and doubt begins to grow. This is why being surrounded by those that keep me in Christ-like accountability and honest self-reflection is key.

The Sandals of Peace and preparation must be ready and *tightened* at all times and I must step without fear of stumbling when in battle, ready to deliver the truth when called upon and provide peace and security through intentional action.
The Shield of Faith is only as big as one grows it.

The size of the shield and its ability to block me and others is directly proportionate to my faith; it defends the whole armor and I practice recognizing and blocking the attacks from the world so as to protect my armor, my very faith itself, by acknowledging worldly attacks, growth and learning opportunities.

The Sword of the Spirit is the word of God-the Bible. Just as a swordsman must practice constantly, so must we as soldiers, for if we do not, its full strength and purpose cannot be wielded and we cannot defend with the Sword of Truth, the word of God, when called. A sword can only be made stronger by having the metal heated and folded, and so too must you utilize the word to heat the fire in your soul for Christ, and then fold the word into your understanding so that you may strengthen your ability to wield the sword of truth with accuracy and precision.

We are all called to be soldiers of Christ, but how that looks and how the armor fits will be different, as will the "boot camp of life" and the training each of us receives. Some may look like fishermen, fishers of men, murderers, collectors, carpenters, prostitutes, kings, queens, bankers, commoners, doctors, lawyers, police, etc. Armor created in the heat of hell will withstand all so there must be an amazing plan.

As a soldier in Christ having faith, I know I must always take action; shining, tightening, hammering, folding, practicing, repairing, growing, dreaming, seeking and moving.
I have been baptized, and redeemed through Christ, I must *act.*
You see, it's not the battle: it's the directive; the goal is to, "Soldier Up," and seek out those who are lost. For as any good soldier knows,

no man gets left behind. We are all brothers and sisters in Christ.

We are not changing people's minds; we are merely there as an example, *through action*, of the ability of God to work through each of our "boot camps," so that we may seek out those who are lost, that we may accomplish the ultimate calling that no man is left behind.

For this body and life were never really meant for us, but for each other, if we stand for and cover each other, then no attack under the sun, by any force, would succeed. I am not as far as I think I should be, yet farther than many, by helping them rise up, learn to grow, care for their armor, fight, and in teaching them how to teach others, I too advance in my walk with Christ.

Well now, isn't teaching what we are called to do?.
It is not about the boot camp; it is about what we did and what did we learned while there. Now that you know the life experiences we have been through were not punishment, but training,
What do you know? What can you teach?

I am sharing with you, my insight of what I have gleaned in my personal boot camp, what I have been *shown* by the other fellow soldiers in Christ who God has blessed me with along my journey, with their insight, strength, leadership, and at times helping to pick me up and pushing me on.

Faith is growing your armor when there is no light, no tools, and no human way to overcome an obstacle. *Faith is* knowing that God will give you the grace and strength to get through it.

Please, dear brother or sister in Christ, know that I am talking to you. It is time to, "Soldier Up". I have faith in you. Start growing your faith, your armor, and join me in doing what we are called to do. Help others determine what *faith is* to them so that they too may grow their armor, establish their calling, and begin a new season of action.

Isaiah 40:31

"31 but they who wait for the Lord shall renew their strength;

they shall mount up with wings like eagles;

they shall run and not be weary;

they shall walk and not faint."

Amen.

Chaplain Mary V. Camp

Mary Vernice Valentine is married to Reverend Thaddeus W. Camp. Mary currently serves as a Sunday School and Bible Study Teacher; President, NV/CA State Congress of Christian Education; Member, Advisory Board of the NBC, USA, Inc. Sunday School Publishing Board (SSPB); Member, International Association of Ministers' Wives and Ministers' Widows. Christian Education Board for the Baptist World Alliance (BWA). She is the first nationally certified Dean of Education for the Nevada/California Interstate Missionary Baptist Convention. Her professional background includes being a Notary Public, Certified Christian Counselor, Certified Executive Administrative Professional, Sign Language and the Deaf Ministry, Black Family Life Institute, Deans and Presidents, Dr. William J. Shaw Master Teachers' Series. A Graduate of six (6) Certificate Programs of National Baptist Convention, USA, Inc., Congress of Christian Education. Mary and her husband are parents to eight children, 15 grandchildren and 15 great grandchildren.

I Have the Scars To Prove It

By Chaplain Mary V. Camp

Being a Christian does not make you exempt from this life's challenges and circumstances. The Apostle Paul wrote in 2 Corinthians 11:23-28 (KJV) "...Are they ministers of Christ? (I speak as a fool) I am more; in labors more abundant, in stripes above measure, in prisons more frequent, in deaths oft. Of the Jews five times received I forty stripes save one. Thrice was I beaten with rods, once was I stoned, thrice I suffered shipwreck, a night and a day I have been in the deep; In journeyings often, in perils of water, in perils of robbers, in perils of mine own countrymen, in perils by the heathen, in perils in the city, in perils in the wilderness, in perils in the sea, in perils among false brethren; In weariness and painfulness, in watchings often, in hunger and thirst, in fastings often, in cold and nakedness. Beside those things that are without, that which cometh upon me daily,..."

My testimony of Faith Is

- ✓ I have sat at the gravesites of my parents, two children, two siblings and a grandchild;
- ✓ I watched my husband battle cancer and survive;
- ✓ I watched my granddaughter's mother battle stage four breast cancer and a double mastectomy, as her younger sister fights MS;
- ✓ I am a survivor of incest;
- ✓ I watched my mother endure brutality, domestic violence and emotional abuse from my father, because she felt she had to, having no education and no income;

✓ I prayed for and with my son as we walked through the justice system for 18 years (he was released September 9, 2016 (GLORY TO GOD);

✓ I pray for strength and the strength of my sisters and brothers in Christ as they care for parents, spouses, children and siblings battling Alzheimer's, mental illness, substance abuse and many other challenges.

Again, being a Christian does not make one exempt for the challenges of this life, those valley experiences. Valley experiences are those where the heartache is so deep or the hardship so difficult that they threaten to overwhelm us. Whether self-inflicted, through other instances or due to the actions of others, we can wander into a painful place, made worse by the knowledge that our fellowship with Him has grown cold (I John 1:6). Whatever the source (unexpected job termination, marital infidelity, betrayal by a friend or attacks within or on the Body of Christ), valley experiences are inevitable. *I have the scars to prove it!* Our strength and courage are tied to concentrating on God's Word. There is no way to hurry through an ordeal marked by emotional or physical distress. Both the trial's depth and length are determined by the Lord's will, but He walks with us and protects us through it. God promises that He will use every valley – even those of our own making – to benefit us (Romans 8:28). Our part is to walk by faith, with eyes firmly fixed on Him, spirits attuned to His presence, and minds trusting in His faithful promises.

Faith is like a muscle, which must be exercised, in order to become strong: just wishing cannot make it happen. Weak faith hopes that God will do what He says, but strong faith knows He is faithful to accomplish all He says He will do. Our lives give testimony and our walk should match our talk. If we say we trust Him and that we have faith, He will bring us through – when trials come we have to step up and walk in faith. When we are buffeted about, we must remember that nothing is too hard for God. He has designed the blueprint for our lives and there is no error in it. When things make no sense and He seems far away; through tears and pain, through

124

heartache and rain – we must say "I will trust you Lord". It is called FAITH.

Faith can be besieged and toppled when its foundation is weakened by unbelief. Fear and uncertainty robs many believers of the peace that the Heavenly Father intends for us to have (John 14:27). Anxiety does not fit who we are in Jesus Christ. By putting our Faith in Him, we have placed our life in the hands of a sovereign God who wants the very best for His children. What do we have to fear when we trust in Him? He knows the root of our anxiety, the best way to calm our heart, and how to turn our weeping into joy (weeping may endure for a night, but joy comes in the morning (Psalm 30:5). He will do all of this without leaving our side, because He loves us deeply and desires to bless us richly.

Scripture teaches that some things only come through prayer and fasting (Matthew 17:21). If you desire your Faith to be strengthened and to draw closer to God, try fasting. Fasting is a spiritual discipline that helps us center our attention on the Lord and discover His will so we may act according to it. Many people fast for many different reasons, different ways, and for different lengths of time. The focus in each case is the same– *to seek God and know His Will*. Fasting does not bring us a quicker answer from God or persuade Him to follow our plan. Instead, it prepares us to see our situation through His eyes and to act on what we learn. Fasting involves a strong desire to hear from God, a period of time to connect with Him, and a willingness to abstain from food or some activity. When it seems like all – H E double hockey sticks [hell], is breaking loose, take time to connect with Him. If the idea intimidates you, remember its purpose is preparation so we might draw closer to God and receive His encouragement and direction.

The morning is like the rudder of our day – how we begin steers our course throughout. I have found that starting the day with God – reading Scripture, meditation, listening to Him for directions – keeps me focused on Him throughout the day. Praying through Scriptures and asking God to speak to our heart about what we read is our privilege as Christians. To grow our faith, we should take full advantage of this privilege.

Contentment is the believer's birthright. Peace is part of the spiritual fruit that is ours when we trust in the Savior (Galatians 5:22); it is an inward serenity that passes all understanding (Philippians 4:7). Jesus lived through conflict with a sense of inner quiet, and because of His indwelling Spirit, that is remarkably calm, belongs to God's children too. That is important because there are times when we come across a problem that has no earthly solution. In situations like those, we learn that self-sufficiency is a lie. We cannot cope alone, but Christ is all we need. The Bible, however, makes it clear that Christians are to be mutually supportive and accountable (James 5:16). Regardless of one's position, everybody is accountable to somebody. And this holds true for the entire family of faith, from the congregation, to the ministers, to Jesus Himself, who serves God the Father. People avoid accountability for various reasons, including pride, ignorance, fear and self-reliance. This is a dangerous approach to life. Our enemy knows our weaknesses and how to exploit them, and will attack us when we are most vulnerable and weak. Read how he came at Jesus in the wilderness (Matthew 4). We can prevail with the support of fellow-believers. There is strength in the Body of Christ.

If we want to hear His voice clearly, we must first address those things that affect how well we are listening. Examine your relationship with God – the vertical MUST be straight. Do you have a clear understanding of who God is? How we view the Lord, changes the way we hear Him. What is your attitude toward God? If we come to the Lord with a proud nature, it is natural that we will not be inclined to hear His voice. Our ability to hear the Lord is directly related to our relationship with Him. Again, the vertical MUST be straight. The Word of God clearly states that whoever believe in Jesus will be saved (John 3:1). This is a choice we must make during our earthly life – there will be no further opportunities once we die.

Without hearing the call to repentance and salvation in Jesus Christ, an unbeliever cannot become part of God's family. But what about those who are believers? Those of us who walk by faith and not by sight. How does a Christian's closeness with God impact his or her listening? It is an issue of identification. Once we receive Christ as Savior, then we certainly have salvation and are eternally secure in Him. But beyond that, God wants us to grow and mature in our faith.

The Bible reveals God's character, records His laws, and explains His expectations for the faithful. In its pages, we can learn about our Father and the kind of life He wants us to lead. "All Scripture is inspired by God and profitable for teaching, for correction, for training in righteousness" (2 Timothy 3:16).

Living by faith almost guarantees hardship! When a person chooses to surrender to God and obey Him no matter what, that believer will suffer at times and be asked to make painful sacrifices. The enemy will say, "it is on – I am going to make you take it back!" When we look at the life of Moses, it was marked by challenge and sacrifice, but more than that, it was shaped by an intimate relationship with God. He spent more than 40 years leading an errant people, interceding for them when they disobeyed God, and calling upon the Lord for rescue when they faced trouble. Every hardship that knocked away his trust in himself, strengthened his faith in the Lord. When a new challenge arose, Moses turned first to God for guidance and provision.

God made the Israelites a promise: release them from slavery, and take them to a land where they would rest and prosper (Deuteronomy 1:1-3; Psalm 105:37; Numbers 13).

To get to the Promised Land they had to go on a journey.

That journey could have taken 11 days – but because the Israelites didn't do what God asked of them, that journey took 40 years.

In Numbers 13, we read that the Israelites were on the verge of entering the promised land, but before they went in, Moses sent in spies to scope it out. Of the twelve that went in – ten came back with reports that while the land was amazing – it was filled with giants and cities that could never be overthrown. After 40 years, having seen God's power at work time and time again, on the verge of receiving God's promise, they still doubted – this time, because of giants in the land and cities with big walls.

What would have happened if the Israelites had done what God asked first?

What if they had made it to the fulfillment of God's promise in 11 days?

I believe that God still has promises for His chosen people – us.

Like the Israelites, He has a journey for us to go on to receive those promises. We can take the 40 year journey – the one where we doubt, get scared by giants or walls that are in the way and take a long time to get there or even prefer to head back to where we came from – or – we can take the 11 day journey, be obedient to what God has called us to do and get there quickly.

Now this might be a simple view – but if the average age we live to is about 70 – if we take the 40 year journey, we only get the chance to fulfill one promise God has for us. But if we choose the 11 day journey – just think about how many times God can use us for His Kingdom purpose.

We all have a unique purpose in God's kingdom plan.

Are you taking the 40 year or 11 day journey?

The Bible says that adversity produces a deeper intimacy with the Lord (I Peter 5:10). Moses' life demonstrates this, and it holds true for you and me today. Hardships are inevitable. We could try doing everything in our power to avoid them, but would probably be unsuccessful. A wiser approach is to meet the challenge and go forward by faith.

God does some extraordinary work in and through each of us who are obedient and willing to trust in Him. He doesn't simply work through people of faith, He transforms us – I have the scars to prove it.   When I look back and think things over, all of my good days, outweigh my bad days….. Many things about tomorrow, I just don't understand. But I know who holds tomorrow and I know He holds my hand.

Healer Iyanla Vanzant says about faith – that when you step out on FAITH – one of two things will happen: either there will be something solid to catch you, or you will be taught to fly!

Chaplain Maria Novello

Maria Novello is the founder of Nevada School of Professional Studies. She helps people advance their skills through education and obtain employment to improve their quality of life. As a business owner she has a desire to "give back" to her community by working with young people and adults. She made a decision that she wanted to have her own company and launched out in faith. She has not looked back and it has been a very fulfilling journey. Maria also hosted her own radio show called "Career and Jobs today". Originally from New York, Ms. Novello relocated to Las Vegas, Nevada. She speaks Spanish & Italian fluently. She is the mother of three children Marc, Marisa and Giovanna. She is an ordained Chaplain with Messages of Faith Ministries, and Co-Author of "Faith Is". Her purpose is to serve all people and lift them up into their destiny. ChaplainMariaNovello@gmail.com

Lights of Love

By Chaplain Maria Novello

Here I am, a girl from Long Island New York, living in Las Vegas. Soon to find out what the Grace of God is all about. On 11/11/11, I was baptized non-denominational Christian from being raised Italian Roman Catholic. My entire family was confused. It took many years for them see the work of God in me. However, my life was about to change forever, and this Grace was about to unfold.

I moved to Las Vegas in blind faith. No job, no family, except myself and children. However, I was blessed to live in the home of my parents. The revelation with this move is that I had been searching for something deep within me from an early age of five. I remember the week I settled in to my home in Las Vegas. I was invited to go to a church by a friend. During that service something amazingly overwhelmed me. I felt the presence of God. The weight and love of our Lord felt so heavy, I literally fell to my knees in tears, and accepted Jesus as my Lord and Savior. That experience was the fulfillment of what I had been looking for. After that point, my life was about to change. My life was no longer mine; my life was about to move from the natural to the supernatural.

When you make this full surrender with God, it is now His job to take full and complete care of you in every detail of your life. There is not an area or detail in your life that God will not be willing to help you out with – no matter how small or trivial you think it may be.

The Holy Spirit is called "the Helper" in the Bible. It is now His job to help you in every single area of your life. Now that you are walking in God's perfect will for your life – God will now be the One to fully guide you. The choice is no longer yours!

So as my faith was growing, I learned to pray, pray and pray some more. I prayed about everything and still do. Every decision I make is based on discerning the Holy Spirit. Through this I went on to start a business and raise my children. However, I noticed I started going through some serious trials. Possibly attacks from the enemy. This is when my faith had to take action. You have choices. You can cower in a corner, cover your head or cry out "poor me." You can shut down any ministry work, business you are doing in the hopes that the enemy will withdraw from attacking you. OR, you can go on the offensive. Counter attack! One thing that works for any kind of attack is to take the helmet of salvation, and the sword of the Spirit, which is the word of God; praying always with all prayer and supplication in the Spirit.

Declare God's Word and his promises over your life. Assert who you are in Christ because of the atoning work of Jesus on the cross. Confidently proclaim that; "No weapon formed against you shall prosper, and every tongue which rises against you in judgment you shall condemn."

And that's what I did.

I had a breast cancer scare, people have hurt me, cheated me, let me down, stole from my bank account, stole from my business, talked bad about me, lied about me, tried to tarnish my name, and even tried to close my business. Just craziness!

And through it all, I leaned on God. People would ask, "How are you so calm?". My answer is, "Life is too short to let peace stealers determine our destiny". I chose to be happy and live at rest. You'll not only enjoy your life more, but I believe and declare God will do more for us. He'll part Red Seas; He'll restore your health, and He'll bring vindication, promotion and the fullness of your destiny. He'll fight your battles if you'll remain at rest!

"The LORD will fight for you; you need only to be still." (Exodus 14:14 NIV) That being the case, we need to drop our hands and relax. We know that God is omniscient (all-knowing), omnipresent (present everywhere), omnipotent (all-powerful), holy, sovereign, faithful, infinite, and good. Acknowledging God implies that we can trust Him and surrender to His plan, because we understand who He is.

Trusting God will take the burden off you. God will now be guiding your steps. You are now operating on a different playing field, where the rules have changed a bit for you.
We need to humbly submit our lives to His sovereign control, and accept that our disappointments don't make Him any less good, loving, or faithful. Sometimes He closes a door because He wants us right where we are.

Remember – God already has your next move all set up and planned out for you. All you have to do is simply wait for His timing to bring it to you! None of the tactics that meant to destroy me has worked! You see, I own a vocational school and I help people advance their skills and help them to get jobs to improve their quality of life. This school was given to me from a vision I had and blessed by God. Meaning he makes it happen on all levels including financially. I can't explain it other than a supernatural Grace upon my life. God just uses me to take care of it and help people. The bigger vision is to setup a Jesus tour and youth home through the money the school makes. This is still in the works. But there is nothing too great for God. My purpose is to serve all people, and lift them up into their destiny. The rest God is in control.

I know the waiting can really get to you, but this is how God develops the fruit of patience and faith in your personality. You simply have to have full faith, trust, and belief that God now has your life completely in His hands, and that He will now bring you're the right place at the right time.

You simply have to learn how to have patience during these waiting periods.

In the meantime, God will make sure to arrange that you have enough money and support coming in to help keep you. This is where you have to learn how to have complete faith in the Lord to do all of this for you.

Trust me, I have been put through the waiting ringer plenty of times, and God has never failed to keep us afloat and open the door to the next step in our walk with Him when the time was right. This is where many Christians really miss the boat with God.
Too many Christians are running their own lives and making their own choices instead of turning the reigns of their life over to God the Father for Him to fully handle.

Only God knows what your true potentials are in this life – and He is the only One who can arrange to have those full potentials maximized and realized in this life!

Some of my favorite scriptures:

3. This first verse will specifically tell you that God now has a definite PLAN and FUTURE set up for your life. This is from the prophet Jeremiah and it is a very popular verse.
    "For I know the thoughts that I think toward you, says the Lord, thoughts of peace and not of evil, to give you a future and a hope." (Jeremiah 29:11)
    Notice the words "to give you." God is going to give you, to bring to you His specific plans and future that He now has in store for your life.

    2. Memorize this next verse. This one is extremely powerful.
    "The steps of a good man are ordered by the Lord … "(Psalm 37:23)
    Another way to look at this is that a step is one day in your life.
    What this means is that God now has each day of your life perfectly planned out for you to the day that you depart from this life. You are now on the yellow brick road with the yellow color being the light of God Himself.

Your job is to now live each day to its fullest, always trying to do the best at whatever God will be calling you to do for Him on that particular day.

If you can learn how to keep this kind of mindset, you will be less likely to be upset when things do not go the way you think they should.

3. Here is another very powerful verse that will tell us that God will provide us with His divine protection, if we are willing to listen to Him and follow His ways.

"But whoever listens to me will dwell safely, and will be secure, without fear of evil." (Proverbs 1:33)

Notice the words "listen to me." God leads – you follow.

This is a very powerful promise for all believers. Many Christians find themselves in one dire circumstance after another, as a result of not listening to God, and doing what He wants them to be doing with their lives.

All of these verses make it very clear that it is God's job to fully guide and direct your steps in this life. And all of this is given to you free of charge.

This is why you can let go and let God.

The Bible also tells us that we can now cast all of our burdens and cares upon the Lord – because it is now His job to take full and complete care of all of us from the moment we fully surrender everything over to Him.

When you start to get too down, or you want to quit, please don't!

In this relationship with God, we have to give ourselves pep talks from time to time, telling ourselves that God has complete control of our entire situation, that the ship is not going to sink, and that our breakthrough will come at the exact time that He has it set up to occur on His timetable.

Until that happens, do what the bible says to do – "Rest in the Lord." What that means is when illness, suffering, difficulties, anguish, confusion, fear, weakness, worry overwhelm, I rest in His Word. His Word enlightens me, strengthens and comforts me. The Word is God.

When it is all said and done, you will look back on all of this and see that you had wasted a tremendous amount of negative energy, since it will have been shown to you that God finally came through for you.

Trust me – I have seen God come through time and time again without fail. There is a saying that many have heard – "God is never late, but He is never early." I am still waiting for the promise of a husband. Singles, be encouraged as I write from a place of surety. I praise the Lord that, whether married or single, "I am fearfully and wonderfully made; marvelous are His works, and that my soul knows very well". Everything God has planned for us from the foundation of the earth will come to pass.

I ask you this, do you feel in need of guidance and direction today? If so, seek wise and godly counsel, ask God for His wisdom and guidance, commit yourself to do His will, and then follow the leading of His Holy Spirit and the truths of His Word. Today my family isn't confused anymore about my faith. They now ask me to pray for them. My business is still doing business. Everything that was taken from me has been restored. My health is good. My three kids are well. And God has led me in sharing in this book!

Have you asked God to come into your heart? Repent of your sins (Acts 3:19), believe in the Lord Jesus (John 3:16; Acts 16:31), and receive Him into your life (John 1:12). We are to change our minds about our sin and about who Christ is, believe Jesus died and rose again, and receive the gift of eternal life by faith.

God has changed my life, he led me to my purpose. Something many people go throughout a lifetime never finding. Being a Christian is more than just talking about the Bible. Live your life in such a way that others see a difference in you. So as you go throughout your life, let others see God's Grace in you! And most importantly save souls! Allow the "Lights of Love" shine though you!

In this city of Las Vegas, the nightlife, glitter and glam, alcohol, drugs, gambling, etc., a city that caters to worldly dreams and desires, I found love. Love which is God. "Where sin increased, grace abounds all the more". Romans 5:20. The light of the gospel is brightest where there is darkness. There is no doubt that my move to Las Vegas is exactly where God intended me to be. Wouldn't it be great at the end of our lives, for God to say, "'Well done, good and faithful servant!'". The Love of God is the Light that directs and guides my steps every day of my life.

God bless the reader of this chapter.

Chaplain Elaine Olson

Elaine Olson and her husband, Ron, were missionaries for several years in Africa. They have ministered in other foreign countries as well as several places in the United States. Elaine graduated from Shiloh Training Institute with honors and was licensed and ordained through them. She also attended the Global School of Supernatural Ministries. She is a chaplain with Messages of Faith Ministries in Nevada. Elaine and her husband have two daughters, nine grandchildren and 16 great grandchildren. She is an intercessor, avid reader, and also enjoys homemaking and interior decorating. Elaine lives with her husband in Henderson, Nevada.

Faith is Spelled R I S K

By Chaplain Elaine Olson

Have you ever seen a mountain goat jump from one cliff to another? There seems to be no hesitation. They just trust in the ability they've had from birth. Sometimes we are faced with something that seems way beyond what we can do in the natural. This is where that faith spelled R I S K comes into being. Just as David stepped out to fight Goliath, when in the natural it seemed absurd, we must take that risk and step out when we've heard the Lord. If David hadn't obeyed, the Israelites would have continued to be in bondage to the Philistines.

The Lord has spoken to my husband and me several times in our lifetime and we have attempted to follow His leading. He has been so faithful to allow us to minister in several countries as well as the United States. I am enclosing one of those times to share how God meets our needs when we step out in faith.

In 1990 we were living in Texas. On January 1st of that year my husband, Ron, and I were having our personal quiet times in different areas of our home. As I was meditating on the Lord, He spoke to me so clearly, "Move to Alaska, I have a work for you there." I was stunned! Personally, I had never wanted to live in a cold climate. I grew up in Iowa and had never liked the cold weather. I pondered this for a while and then went to speak to my husband. He thought it was wonderful. He said, "Twist my arm!" We didn't speak to anyone about this for a week, but prayed and listened to Holy Spirit. He kept confirming it in our hearts.

We then shared it with our two daughters and their husbands. Our son-in-law, Tim, had wanted to go to Alaska for a couple of years, but every time we prayed about it the doors closed. Now he said, "That is confirmation for me. I'm heading to Alaska." A few weeks later he took off for Alaska to find work, before coming back for his family. Our other daughter and her family headed to Florida where they went to help birth a church.

As we continued to pray, the Lord spoke to my husband audibly at work, the word Homer. There was no one around him so he knew it had to be the Lord. As we searched a map of Alaska, we found that there was a town called Homer at the end of the Kenai Peninsula. Now we knew where we were headed but when and how? We just had an old car, and we knew that it would not get us there. As I prayed, I heard the Lord say, "Go to Tyler Ford." Ron had commented that he would like a white car with red interior, standing for purity and the blood of Jesus. We did not have the money to buy outright. We asked God what we should do. We felt that he said to have a car payment of around $200.00 a month.

Off to Tyler Ford we went. Sure enough there was a new white Ford with red interior. The price had been reduced from $11,200 to $7,200. We finally got the price down to $206.00 a month. It was dark when the salesman took us out to the car. Ron asked if it had rear defrosters, knowing we'd need them in Alaska. The man said it didn't but we could put in a kit. Ron and I were on either side of the car when the man opened the trunk. He exclaimed, "It has rear defrosters and they weren't on the list so I can't charge you for them." At that time, Ron felt an arm go around his shoulders and whisper in his ear, "This is only the beginning." There was not a person close to him.

Now we had the transportation we needed. *Now, Lord, when do you want us to leave?* There were several people who thought we were crazy. They said that they knew of people who had gone to Alaska and had to return because they couldn't make it. Others said we should get a good job, save money and maybe in five years we'd be able to afford to go. As we sought the Lord, He said leave the 1st of June that year. We had no savings and no credit cards, but we said, "Okay, Lord, we're in your hands. We're making that jump and trusting You to catch us."

After checking with God to see if we could go to Florida first to see our kids, we filled our car with what it could hold and headed to Florida. While there we went to a Charles and Francis Hunter seminar. Ron's back was giving him a little trouble so he went forward for prayer. A couple prayed for his back. When his back was healed, they asked if he needed prayer for anything else. He said that God was sending us to Alaska and that we could use prayer for that. After praying for him, they handed him a check for $500.00. They said, "This is from the Lord and there is more where that came from." That couple sent us a check monthly for two years. Ron was astounded, because he'd not said anything about needing finances. That's the faithfulness of our God!

After a few weeks with our kids in Florida, we headed to Iowa for a family reunion. From there we went to Minnesota where our Pastor's in- laws lived. They graciously invited us to stay a couple of days. That evening they had a prayer meeting in their home. The group ministered to us, prayed and prophesied over us. One word given to us was that there was a native woman that was praying and somehow we were a part of her prayer. Before we left they gave us

$500.00 for our ministry. Again, we had not mentioned any need for finances, but our Father takes care of His kids!

As we had been traveling, we asked the Lord what we would be doing in Alaska. He said, "You are to build the church through prayer." We knew that He had led us this far, so He would take care of working out all the details.

Our next stop was Montana, where we had attended Bible School. There was a camp meeting going on the week that we were there. Again, we were ministered to. One couple gave us $100.00. We headed up through Canada and arrived in Alaska on July 25, 1990 with $100.00 left. We marveled at how our Father God took care of us as we obeyed Him. We believe that if we would have waited until we had enough to go on our own, we'd have probably never gone.

When we arrived in Homer, we knew no one. We were there a couple of days when we met a couple who knew of a native lady that needed someone to live in her apartment in her house. She was blind and needed someone to be able to take her places, etc. She was not able to charge rent because she was being helped by the native association. We lived there for two years rent free and was able to minister to her in many ways.

Through friends, we met Mary Glazier, who was over the Intercessors of Alaska. There were intercessory groups in villages all over Alaska. They would come together in Anchorage once a year for a conference with well-known prophetic speakers. She felt that the Lord had sent us to Alaska to start an intercessory group in Homer. She held meetings there and installed us as intercessory leaders for that area. For over ten years we held intercessory prayer meetings in our home every week. People and even pastors from six different churches came together to pray. Pastors invited us into their churches during the week to pray. They also asked us to hold a pastors' conference for them. Churches came together a couple of times a year to hold united services in the high school gym. God moved mightily in those years. We felt privileged to be a part of what He was doing.

In the summer of 1995, a prophet from Georgia came to Homer. He prophesied over me and said, "That was Me who called you to the cold country five years ago in January." It was so precious of the Lord to confirm to me what I had heard from Him on January 1st 1990.

Sometime you may need the, Faith of God, Mark 11:22, to make that jump from a spiritual cliff. If you have heard God, you can trust that He will catch you! I Samuel 15:22 states, To obey is better than sacrifice. Philippians 4:13 says, I can do all things through Christ who strengthens me. Sometimes walking in faith is difficult, but if we take that R I S K, we will be blessed beyond measure, and we'll be able to fulfill the call God has put in our lives.

Chaplain Rachael Richardson

A native Nevadan who with a passion and reputation for being an Ambassador of Christ is redirecting at-risk youth away from a life of crime for the purpose of guiding them into their God given destiny. Chaplain Rachael's transparency and genuine transformation provide Hope for the seemingly hopeless. Her unwavering commitment to helping endangered youth keep from extinction is what has earned her the respect of those from the Whitehouse to the Jailhouse. Chaplain Rachael takes time to share her expertise of both the hard knock life & the "law" to people all over the nation, especially youth who think they're invincible & those who have been given the responsibility of ensuring the youth of today become the leaders of tomorrow such as parents, teachers, employers and law enforcement alike. Rachael & her husband Channing are ordained Chaplin's with Messages Of Faith Ministries & long time members of Victory Outreach Las Vegas.

Molestation to Murder, It All Matters

By Chaplain Rachael Richardson

"But without faith it is impossible to please Him: for he must believe that He is, and that He is a rewarder of them that diligently seek Him"
Heb.11:6

Is this God's definition of a "reward?" This was all I could think of during the early hours on that fateful Sunday in May. I was lying flat on my back on a thin piece of plywood covered by an even thinner mattress, wearing a white plastic jumpsuit staring at the ceiling of the Washoe County Detention Center's suicide observation cell. After being interrogated for over 8 hours for accidentally killing a family member, I was booked on first-degree murder with the use of a deadly weapon!

I've heard it said "Faith is the assurance that God will do what He said He will do even when all evidence says contrary."

However, in living a life of a murderous harlot I wasn't sure that God would do what He said He would do, if I didn't do what I said I would do. Like most people, as a child I went to church, and said the "sinner's prayer" only to sin continuously, and the sins seemed to keep getting bigger the more I said "the prayer." Then AFTER I missed it AGAIN, there I was like "God please forgive me. If you get me out of the consequences of this, I promise I will go to church, sing in the choir, clean the church, anything God just get me out of this" Even if you've NEVER stepped foot in a church I'm sure you've used a "spare tire" prayer. Then sure enough a modern day "miracle" occurs and off we go like nothing ever happened. Sunday comes and we might even go to church but it's not long before we've completely forgot about the promise we made to God and at times even the situation God rescued us out of.

As I lay there watching the clouds pass over it's as if I saw my life being played out on a big screen, seeing how all of the choices I've made and promises I've broken to God finally landed me right where I deserved to be, NOWHERE. I'm 21 years old, I've spent my whole life up until this very day looking for love in all the wrong places, with all the wrong people, doing all the wrong things. I was pretty much raised in the church when I was with my grandparents so I should have known "better" yet the church was never raised up in me. I had no idea we were "the separated ones, called out and hand chosen to proclaim liberty to captives. " All I saw were a bunch of hypocrites who claim they loved God but couldn't stand me.

My mom's family was white; they had an infamous prestige in the state of Nevada, and in the 70's couldn't be ruined with a black grandchild. My father's side of the family believed my mother was the devil because she had blonde hair and blue eyes, and must have put a "spell" on my dad in order for him to be with her. Yet both sides behaved extremely religious. Not accepting me made perfect sense, seemingly they loved a god that obviously didn't accept me either, who was going to allegedly send me to hell's fire if I wore pants, cut my hair, or wore makeup. Their other god required me on my knees, singing hymns, and baptized me by drizzling water on my forehead. Nonetheless, both sides agreed that their god would absolutely send me to hell for   killing myself or anyone else.

Is their God is supposed to be same God who has saved my butt in so many "sinful" situations (like when I got pregnant at 15 by a gang member and God allowed me to hear my daughter's heartbeat on an abortion clinic table. What the nurse called a "sack of multiplying cells" God called "fearfully & wonderfully made." "Cells" don't have heartbeats, humans do) just for me to go back to my vomiting sins again? At this point I'm so confused. In my mind I see the god that others have told me about, the lightning finger god who waits for me to do something wrong so he can send me to hell with no remorse. Yet, in my heart I feel the love of a Father I never knew. One that has protected and provided for me and mine time and again, (like when I was leaving my son's father, who was a pimp & I fell asleep behind the wheel totaling my car but neither of my 2 children or myself were hurt, AT ALL) and He's asked for nothing in return but for me to trust Him.

Psalms 91:11-12-For He will order His angels to protect you wherever you go. They will hold you up with their hands so you won't even hurt your foot on a stone.

It was almost as if I heard the devil saying "when you were my child I never let you get caught selling dope or even driving drunk. But now you are a child of God and look at you!" I tried to ignore the racing thoughts but I couldn't seem to shake them. Was God upset that I was drinking and partying last night? I had been doing so well for over 3 months, when I left my son's father it was because I wanted to be right before God.

I had a 15 yr old cousin tragically murdered by her step dad, since I was going to the funeral I thought there's no better time than now to leave him, "OK God I trust You"
I was diligently trying to live for God, was this my reward? I was rewarded much better for doing the wrong things, or so I thought.

147

My life seemed to be playing out before my very eyes; I can see God in every situation.

My grandmother realized I was black from the time I was born and dropped me; God caught me up safely in the palm of His hand. When I was being molested from the ages of 6-9, and raped at 13, God provided a way of escape. At 16 when I was homeless about to give birth, God allowed a total stranger to take me, my drug addicted mom, her addict boyfriend into her home. When I was driven into the woods with a knife to my neck and then to the graveyard, it was God who turned that guy's heart to let me live. I also saw how the Lord allowed me to get into situations to cry out to Him. He knew I'd be the only child my mom would ever get pregnant with (though she tried so many other times by so many men.) He allowed my mom to run off time and again, and He opened the door for me to stay with the McAlister's. And although they weren't religious they showed me the love of Christ, as they rearranged and laid down their whole lives that I might never have to go into the system.

 I saw how seeds of doubt had been planted in my mind about how God wasn't real, if He was why do bad things happen, such as my 15yr old cousin being murdered by her step-dad who was a pastor, or kids getting raped and more. People have choices and free will. "I came to be an example and a ransom for you, because I love you. The thoughts I have for you are to give you a future, a hope, not to harm or hurt you.
I know the end from the beginning, I will see you through to the end if you Trust ME. Taste & see that I AM good. Said the Lord"

For the first time in my life I didn't just want to "say a prayer" I wanted to know the Creator of the Universe that I was saying prayers to. It was right there in that jail cell cold, alone, afraid, confused that I didn't say a prayer simply out of my mouth I cried out with a loud

148

voice from the depths of my heart and said "God I need you I have nothing to bring to You. I have nothing to offer You, not only do I have nothing, I am nothing!". Nobody has EVER wanted me except for those who I had just devastated by accidentally killing the only son of the woman I call grandma, the only brother of the women who have opened their homes for the last 21 years to me, women who I call my aunties! And the uncle of my cousins who always treated me like their sister, MY UNCLE, the only man who bought my daughter diapers and never asked for anything in return.

I asked, "what about his SIX children God, the youngest is not even a month old she will never know the amazing father she had! Oh God, All I've ever wanted was to be the mom I never had, so my kids would never feel the way I have always felt, unloved. So IF You are real and You really love me like You say You do, PROVE IT, take my life right now because I can't live like this another minute!" Though I was hoping to breathe my last breath right there in that jail cell, clearly that didn't happen. But God did take my life as I knew it and He showed me why Jesus Christ paid for EVERY foul, nasty, despicable, vial, unthinkable sin I had committed from gossiping to murder, a sin is a sin. In God's eyes sins all are equal and equally paid for by The Blood that was shed on the cross & that "karma" was not coming to get me, I've been forgiven!!

The more I read the Holy Bible, God's Basic Instructions Before Leaving Earth, the more I saw how God knew His people would not keep their promises. Yes, it upsets God. Yes, it breaks His heart but He kept and still keeps His promises anyway! I have seen over and over when I was totally faithless, God remained faithful! But why? That's when I really began to ask the Lord "what is FAITH really? Romans 4:5-says "But to him that worketh not, but believeth on Him that justifieth the ungodly, his faith is counted for righteousness." Faith is not blind, the Lord has a proven track record of being

149

trustworthy not because of what we do or don't do but because of who He is! He knew that I would be used to reach people all over the world with the message of Hope that "if you're not dead, it's not over!" It doesn't matter what you've done, God will cause it to work out for good and for His purpose.

I was eventually convicted of 2nd degree murder with the use of a deadly weapon but never saw the inside of Mclure women's prison (AKA Smiley road) until I went in with my church Victory outreach to preach Hope to the women. I was on my way to pick up 400 ecstasy pills to kill myself AFTER I was miraculously let out of jail, but I got off the wrong exit going to my dope dealer's house and Victory Outreach was there having a car wash! I wasn't looking for God, I was running from Him. I saw how He used me in the jail for over 220 days. I saw how He set me free, and not the jury, yet when I was released I also saw that I could not understand the fact of my family STILL loving me.

I wanted them to hate me like I hated me; therefore in order for me to cope I started using drugs BAD! Yet God met me at that car wash and I've been at VO ever since. Victory Outreach was filled with "sinners" like me, more importantly sinners who saw the "saint" in me and they invested time into my life. When one of my children was molested by neighborhood kids, Sister Cece sat with me at the hospital and came to my house with me so I wouldn't do anything regrettable.

I met my husband at VO and he is a product of the men's recovery home. We didn't even kiss until we were married. I remember my grandma would say "if they love you they will wait." To which I replied, "if I make them wait they will leave" Well grandma, you were right AGAIN. My mom has been clean and sober for over 10 years and has lived with us and helped with the kids. We have a total of six kids, ages 24, 23, 19, 9, 6, and two. When I got pregnant with our son, Channing Jr. we were told he had Trisomy 13 and the Dr. even went as far as to get a "medical termination" approved through our insurance. I wasn't always sure if I had made the right decision by NOT "terminating" the pregnancy but I was sure that God was a Healer and I knew He was more trustworthy than the doctor whose only option was death. Channing Jr. is now a happy healthy 6 yr. old, and he's the only child who received a 4D ultrasound for free.

I have the privilege of working with the youth today, helping them avoid the mistakes I once made, and since I KNOW now that the Lord doesn't ask us to have faith in the unseen, I tell the youth of His wondrous works and remind them God isn't a respecter of persons, since He did it for me, He will do it for you. He just asks us to look at what we've seen so far and trust that if He took care of us when we couldn't even take care of ourselves, how much more then, when we allow Him to drive as we ride shotgun? He qualifies the called, He doesn't call those who think they are qualified because then they try to take the glory that only belongs to Him. Faith is knowing what God has done in the past, and knowing He's still at work even when we don't see a future.

We may not know how God is going to do something, yet, we can be confident that He will get it done, one way or the other, or maybe another way that we had not even dreamed about.

"For My thoughts are not your thoughts, neither are your ways My ways," says the Lord. For as the heavens are higher than the earth, so are My ways higher than your ways, and My thoughts than your thoughts." Isaiah 55:8-9

Chaplain Dennis Smith

Dennis began his business career in 2006, after completing his MBA in October 2005. He took a break from his corporation in 2009 to serve in Baghdad and Al Kut, Iraq as an overseas contractor. In 2012 he became a chaplain (called during a church service) and has since been ordained. Dennis is currently enrolled for his 2nd Master's degree (professional counseling) with the goal of ultimately earning a doctorate and becoming established as a licensed psychologist. This man is an energetic and creative person who approaches life and career with enthusiasm for growth in wholehearted living. That same energy feeds his primary focus of serving God. Dennis finds creative ways to make the process fun and enjoyable for those around him. He is available as a National Speaker, and can be reached by email at: DSmith@DRSmithCM.com, or LinkedIn at: Dennis Smith, MBA, Chaplain.

Perseverance After Childhood Trauma

By Chaplain Dennis Smith

This is a real life true story about my personal experience with childhood trauma, in the form of physical abuse. By the way; please allow me to first say that this book is being written to help, and not to hurt anyone. There have been many nudges over the years to tell this story. It is time. This manuscript is being written with a child's prayer, and with experience, strength and hope, to encourage at least one of you out there who will relate to these shared occurrences, and the subsequent faith-filled perseverance. With the type of family dynamics that existed back then, and to some degree still do, it will not surprise me when this book brings some mixed emotions and even possible negative feedback as a result of this being published. That's ok. Many families have had secrets for years, and there comes a time when we are only as sick as our secrets.

"It's going to be alright." You may be surprised or even puzzled by that statement within context. It happens to be a powerful emotional statement that has for years been one of my favorites. First things first. God brought me into this world in 1957, with parents that included a former Catholic Nun and a protestant former Golden Gloves boxer. To most observers, the eventual family of seven appeared to be one of those All-American types. This author's place among this family happened to be that of first born son. My initial memories are from the age of two (puffing a cigarette…more on that later) and having my first sip of alcohol at a very young age of three (wanting to emulate my Dad) in an attempt to model my hero. These initial recollections were nice memories. In fact, I only have fond memories until the age of five, and the most painful reflections have been from the age of seven. Of course, one of my most cherished experiences was also in 1964 (at age seven).

As a five-year-old, one day my parents were having one of those, what we later referred to as a high-volume-discussion. Entering the room un-noticed, my young ears heard Dad say to Mom, "I have told you a hundred times, they made a mistake at the hospital with Dennis, and he is not our boy!" Try to imagine hearing that from your hero...can you? And, then consider the feelings of who then are my parents, and where are they? Eventually some of those thoughts and emotions were identified with feeling abandoned and adopted as a result of someone else's choice.

 At age seven my Grandmother Smith (a prayer-warrior in a protestant denominational church) introduced me to the Bible; to the daily devotional booklets known as "Our Daily Bread;" and to Jesus. I had now reached an understanding of the Gospel message and had made a personal decision to accept and live for Christ. Yes, this was one of my favorite memories. However, then all hell broke loose. At seven years of age I was attending a private parochial school and walking one mile each way. One day, upon returning home from school, I met Mother just inside the house, and she was in a fit of rage.

Just inside the back door were the stairs leading to the basement. To this day, it is my belief that the devil had gotten a hold of her that afternoon. I was pushed down the stairs; she rushed to catch up with me; and then she angrily began choking the life out of me. This was years before ever hearing or reading about so-called out of body experiences. Keep in mind that to the seven-year-old, it was akin to feeling as if things were upside down or were going crazy. In hindsight, I recall looking down upon this scene and witnessing my mother letting go with both hands, as she gasped in disbelief because her son had stopped breathing. She ran back upstairs!

At this point, everything was different, such as from the part where you (usually) read about how others have seen bright lights and a tunnel, (typical out-of-body story from others) etc. All I remember is hearing a very warm, comforting and loving voice, asking where I wanted to go. My choice was to return, and the voice stated, "Everything is going to be alright." Next, I was back coughing and trying to breathe. Soon after this happened, mom didn't want me to look in a mirror, and she kept me home from school for what seemed like several days (due to strangle marks on my neck). When I did return to school the explanation was that my throat was in a lot of pain.

Apparently, this experience prompted me to begin sleep-walking. Sometime after, in what seemed to have been the same month and year; my Dad had come home late at night (working two jobs), and he thought we had a home-intruder. Dad, by the way was a big strong man, and a former golden gloves boxer. He threw me up against a living room wall, of which the body-slam abruptly woke me up. My thought was that a monster was attacking me! Upon sliding down the wall to the floor and catching a clear glimpse from a street light shining into the living room window, my next thought was that the monster was my own father! Why? God, why is this happening? Was this all because the hospital had made a mistake and I really didn't belong to this family?

Later on in life when re-reading scripture, and more specifically the book of John, chapter ten and verse ten, the scenarios made more sense. *"The thief comes only to steal and kill and destroy; I came that they may have life, and have it abundantly* (John 10:10 NASB). This scripture is Jesus speaking to both you and me. The more I learn, grow, love and serve...the more my belief increases that it was His [Jesus] voice that spoke to me as a seven-year-old hurting child. My initial belief in 1964 was that it had to be a visiting angel!

Granted, these were only two isolated incidents. However, the verbal and physical abuse, to a lesser degree, continued occasionally for years (just nothing quite as damaging). At age ten, Dad, during a fit of rage, grabbed the back of my head with his large hand and slammed my face into the kitchen table. To this day my two front teeth are chipped from the incident, and the memory was buried until a dentist questioned me in 2010, asking how long these teeth were chipped.

Life kept happening; situational circumstances were stuffed; mom occasionally tried to convince others and me that there was a habit of mine towards making up stories. Meanwhile, I kept praying and forgiving. Unfortunately, these were losses that needed to be grieved, and nobody taught us back then how to adequately face circumstances that required grief recovery. You may be asking yourself, what do you mean? These real abusive actions brought about loss of faith and loss of trust. Seriously. I cannot begin to express the type of emotional and psychological pain experienced, though this book is a written attempt to find a way to help others who have gone through anything similar. Psalm 46:10 has often brought comfort and peace, with the words, *"Be still, and know that I am God"* (New King James Version).

Dad seemed to grow bitterer towards me, and Mom spent six months in a mental hospital for depression. Fortunately, the medical profession has learned more in recent years, and the fact that a former Nun having five kids (from 1956-1963) after getting married at the age of 20! Just imagine the post-partum issues. Our family soon moved outside the city when I was ten, and we began attending a public school. At this large school district out in the country, my new friends were mostly Christians. Was this coincidental? Looking back, nobody could convince me otherwise that this was an answered prayer. The blessings never seemed so evident until looking back several years later as an adult living 2000 miles away from that county. This was truly a child's answer to prayer, indeed.

Eventually, my Dad was persuaded to allow me (as a teen) to leave the Catholic Church. It was my belief that he would understand, since he was born and raised a protestant. Six weeks after leaving the church of my childhood, a phone call arrived from an adult requesting me to speak at a large catholic school. They scheduled me to be a guest speaker for a high school senior religion class. This turned out to be an opportunity for God to bless me as a teacher-preacher-evangelist. The school never invited me back because too many of these seniors were now ready to leave the catholic faith! Hopefully this church is now doing a better job of teaching the truth from scripture. Don't get me wrong here, as my heart still loves the Catholic Church. After all, it is part of my family heritage and they remain on my prayer list.

Over the years there have been a number of people and circumstances that have helped me heal from the childhood trauma. To all of you, I am forever grateful, especially for helping me know that the childhood issues were not my fault; and for gently leading me back to faith and relationship with my Creator. Life has brought a mixed-bag of blessings and sorrows, and my experiences have included divorce; alcohol addiction; graduate business school with high honors (3.87gpa); two start-up companies; two motorcycle accidents in California with subsequent health issues, medical bills and bankruptcy; and a life of recovery.

Upon returning from Iraq in 2009 as a contractor, there was a calling to chaplaincy. After a number of years volunteering as a hospital chaplain, the Nevada Chaplaincy led me through the ordination process. Though there is a love in my heart for hospital and hospice chaplain work; in recent years there has been a new direction, and I am now enrolled in another Master's degree (professional counseling) with the goal of ultimately earning a Doctorate degree and being established as a licensed psychologist.

God is good…all the time. I have learned to greatly appreciate the bible verse Romans 8:28, which states, *"And we know that God causes all things to work together for good to those who love God, to those who are called according to His purpose"* (New American Standard Bible). During challenging moments this verse always encourages me to keep persevering, and it provides hope regardless of the current circumstances. When looking back at earlier mentioned situations, this verse was truly a source of strength. I can only imagine where this life would be now, had I either not taken the detour into alcohol dependence, or chose to seek help sooner. Still, the best is yet to come, and though life still happens, there is an inner gratitude beyond anything I could have ever dreamed of.

Moreover, there still seems to remain room for healing and growth, and this authoring effort (Faith Is…) has already proven to be part of that process. "Trust the process" is a viable solution of sorts. For years I was afraid to discuss my past with anyone, and the habit of stuffing emotions and feelings continued. This developed into increasing "pain and pretending." My pain had been too overwhelming to deal with and the weight of pretending that everything was alright had been getting unbearable. My solution (as previously referenced) slowly turned to alcohol, because of the affects and how it generated the feelings and allusion that my life really was ok or better.

Unknowingly to myself, this pattern of dysfunctional decision(s) was leading me further away from my child-found faith. For the longest time my drinking wasn't occurring that often and yet that too, became a form of self-deception. Whenever I did drink, my behavior suffered, and people were injured from my selfish choices. It became a moment of clarity that my alcohol abuse was a personal attempt towards numbing the deeply stuffed hurt and pain

Looking back over the years there was also a pattern of trying to achieve certain successes in order to feel better; patterns of getting my hands on a drink of alcohol and then experiencing behavior that prompted others to respond in disbelief; patterns of running from a fear and belief that if I ever truly got to know myself, there would be a painful discovery of learning what it was about me that triggered the abusive habit from both parents. There was also a nagging mindset of wondering who my real parents really were, and thoughts of why they abandoned me to these people that often didn't want me in their lives.

Finally, there was always the presence of God, wherever my paths wandered. Perhaps my Baptist friends were right in suggesting that, "once saved always saved." Or, maybe God was keeping watch over me with help from His angels, and not only because He had mentioned that "everything was going to be alright." One time in a nightclub a lady approached me, asking if this was really me. Next, she stated, "Oh! I thought you were supposed to be a Christian!" Yes, the conviction was heavy at that moment, and it lingered for quite some time. Fortunately, I followed the direction that delivered me to a peace beyond all human understanding. There often seemed to be a Christian person whom was crossing paths with me, and working as a messenger of sorts. Eventually these friends helped prepare me for my future spouse. A value added gift of grace that followed was meeting my wife Ria, and we were married in 2008.

God has used Ria to further bless me in a multitude of ways. She now knows me better than anyone, with the exception of God alone. Perhaps a complete book will follow, of which will do more to help others come to terms with their own fears. Speaking of fears, this reminds me of a scripture from the book of Daniel. *Then He said to me, "Do not fear, Daniel [Dennis], for from the first day that you set your heart to understand, and to humble yourself before your God, your words were heard; and I have come because of your words."* – Daniel 10:12

If you have found yourself relating to this portion of my story, or perhaps something similar; if you are feeling pain, please be encouraged and know that God is there right now for your need. Mathew 8:27 is an example of Christ Jesus' miracle power over nature (and everything else). Jesus is God and He can calm any storm in our lives, and we can place our complete trust in Him. Feel free to contact me if I can be of any help and/or prayer.

Chaplain Leon G. Stevens

Leon was born and raised in Sacramento, California September 14, 1946. He served four years in the United States Air Force. Leon is retired and living in Las Vegas, Nevada. He has been married for forty years and has three children and four grandchildren. He is an ordained Chaplain with Message of Faith Ministry and a Minister at Southern Hills Baptist Church in Las Vegas, Nevada.

He has a passion for the spreading the Gospel of Jesus Christ and sharing God's word wherever and whenever he can. He is the author of "One Nation Under God: A Factual History of America's Religious Heritage."

What God Has Done In My Life

By Chaplain Leon G. Stevens

2 Corinthians 5:17
[17] Therefore if any man be in Christ, he is a new creature: old things are passed away; behold, all things are become new

Christians are brand-new people on the inside. The Holy Spirit gives them a new life. We are not reformed; rehabilitated, or reeducated…we are new creations. I am telling you this is so true!

I was not raised in a Christian family. I had no religious example in my life at all. So I went through life not knowing our Lord, walking in darkness.

Before I was saved, instead of studying the Word of God, I was studying the World of Satan. Thinking I would write a book someday, I was researching the occult; like séances, witchcraft, Satan worship, and anything else satanic.

My wife, Sandie, regularly attended church, inviting me along and continuously praying for me. I went three times and complained about it all the way home.

Sandie and I had been married for 32 years when we moved to a community quite a distance from the church she had been attending. One Saturday she said she wanted to find a new church with or without me. I said I had been thinking about it for a while and that I would like to go with her. She responded, "don't do it for my sake, do it for yourself". I said it would be.

We went church hopping trying to find the right one for us. While driving home from the 7th church visit, Sandie was very upset. She was in tears and cried out to God, "You finally got him to want to go to church and now we can't find one! Please tell me where you want us to go, give us some kind of sign!".

When we got home we found a tract on our gate from Southern Hills Baptist Church (SHBC) in Las Vegas, Nevada.

We started going to services August 2, 2009 (The churches 5th Anniversary). As soon as I entered the building I knew I was supposed to be there. It felt like home. This really was the first church I willingly attended in my adult life.

At this time, I was 63 years old and I didn't know God.... Oh, I knew who He was, and I knew He was there, but I didn't KNOW Him. That is until I went to Southern Hills Baptist Church. The love and caring I found there softened my heart and allowed me to find our Lord and Savior Jesus Christ.

Sandie had been going to church most of her life but was never taught about salvation until we started going to SHBC. We both accepted Christ as our Savior on August 18, 2009. Once I accepted Christ as my Savior, things changed dramatically for me.

We all know that God is the Divine Healer. We also know that He doesn't heal everyone. We don't know why; He just doesn't. The moment I accepted Christ as my   Savior I was healed.

163

I was diagnosed with degenerative arthritis in my spine. I was always in pain and had trouble sleeping. The night of my salvation I had the first good night sleep since I don't know when and I have been pain free ever since! I still don't know why He healed me and He won't heal others. I do know it's all part of His plan.

I went to the doctor shortly after that and told her what had happened. She said "Many things can happen through faith." My Pastor told me if the pain comes back, don't think God has turned His back on me, because that won't be the case. So far the pain has not returned.

Besides being healed, there are several distinct ways the Holy Spirit has been with me and helped me. One, before I was saved, I couldn't talk in front of people. Even three people was a crowd to me and I couldn't speak. A few months after I was saved, I believe it was January 2010, I gave my first testimony at church in front of the whole congregation. It was amazing to me. I had no fear, no nerves. I felt very comfortable in front of everyone. That was the Holy Spirit working on me, I am sure. Then the Lord put on my heart the desire to spread His word.

The first way God has worked through me is preaching. Remember before I was saved I was terrified to speak in front of people. Well the Lord has seen fit to bless me with the gift of speaking. I was given an opportunity to speak at Acacia Spring Assisted Living Home. My first sermon was March 5, 2011. Both Pastor Teis, our lead pastor and Pastor Coombes, our program pastor, guided me through the process. They encouraged me and helped me with the message. I had spoken there 4 times up to the end of that year. In December, I told Pastor Teis the Lord had put on my heart to preach more in the new year. Without hesitation, Pastor Teis asked if I would like to take over the ministry at Acacia Springs. Of course I said yes.

Even before I started this ministry, another opportunity to serve the Lord came up. A friend of ours has been helping out at a place called Vintage Park, a memory care facility. She was told they were in need for some spiritual guidance and worship service there, and our friend told them about me. I was approached about the idea and immediately knew I had to say yes. I talked to Pastor Teis about it and he said to go ahead with the blessing and aid of SHBC.

I continued to think about this additional ministry and wondered if I really should do it. I said to myself. "What if I just say no, what if I just walk away, they don't know me and I haven't really promised I would do it." Then a very strong thought came into my head "Remember what happened to Jonah." That was enough to convince me that this is indeed a ministry I must do.

 Sandie, my devoted partner in these ministries and I, now hold worship services and share the Word of God at both of these places the first and third Sundays of each month. I look forward to expanding this ministry to other facilities like these in the future.

Gotta love God's sense of humor. Before I was saved and since I was getting older, I didn't want to be around older people. I guess I thought it might rub off. Well, when I was save,d I think the Lord said "Guess what. You're old so deal with it!" And He set me on the path to minister to the "old folks."

I also am fortunate to be able to preach periodically at Las Vegas Rescue Mission. Wherever I go, it is such a blessing to be able to preach the Word of our Lord to those who cannot go to a traditional place of worship.

I found out that when the Lord asks you to do something for Him, He will provide what is necessary to accomplish it. The Lord provided the tools I needed to spread His word. Someone donated many Bible commentaries by various authors, and related books to SHBC. These books help to explain and understand the Word of God and to aid in preparing messages. Pastor Jason offered them to me and of course I jumped at the chance. To me, they are a gold mine of information. I thank God for the opportunity to learn more about His word, and to be able to preach His Word with more knowledge and confidence.

Soon after we began going to SHBC, we had a fellowship gathering at our home. As we were going home from church, she said, "O,h by the way, at the gathering you are expected to give some sort of devotional. It should only be about 10 or 15 minutes." I panicked! I had no idea what I was going to do. I had never done anything like this in my life. I ask her what in the world could I do.

At the time, I was writing a novel about the Civil War so Sandie said "why don't I talk about the Civil War and how it relates to the Bible and to God." I thought for a moment and then all of a sudden it came to me. I had heard a short time before, President Obama make a startling claim that "The United States of America is not a Christian nation." That really set me off! I guess nothing gets hotter than a new Christian that's on fire for the Lord.

I decided right then I would make my devotional proof that we are indeed a Christian nation. I can only say that the Lord put that thought on my heart and I knew I must follow through with it.

I did the devotional (it was actually about 25 minutes). That was the first time I had spoken in front of any kind of group. (This was before I had given my testimony   in January.)

I had a dream one night and I usually don't put too much thought about what I dream. I dreamt I was giving my devotional to a very large faceless audience. What could that mean? Of course! A faceless audience would be readers of a book!! I believe now the Holy Spirt came to me and the revelation to me was astounding. I expanded my devotion it into what is now my book "One Nation Under God: The Factual History of America's Religious Heritage".

I had been writing for about 17 months plus working full time. I thought to myself, I just need more time to concentrate on my book, so I prayed for more time to write.

Shortly after, the VP of the company I worked for came to me and said I was to be laid off due to lack of work. The first thing that popped into my head was "Praise the Lord I can finish my book!"

As I worked on my book I really believe the Holy Spirit was working with me. I found things in my research that I may not have otherwise found and words just flowed as I was typing. I worked another 5 months on the book. That is 5 months without a pay check. In April of 2011 I said "I am finished!". The very next day Ed, the owner of the company, emailed me and asked me to come back to work, with a promotion and pay raise! Needless to say I said yes. I stayed there until I retired in March 2016. I really believe it was divine intervention that was at work.

Once the book was finished I prayed and asked my church to pray to have endorsements from some prominent people in this fields of history and religion. After four months of waiting and praying I received them. They are from David Barton of Wallbuilders (known as America's Historian), Dr. David Gibbs, of Christian Law Association, Dr. Paul Chappell of West Coast Baptist College and Dr. David Teis, founder and lead pastor of Liberty Baptist Church in

Las Vegas, Nevada.

I had hoped to have my books on the bookshelves by Christmas, but the endorsements held me up. My next goal was to have it out in the middle of election season. So I guess God decided election season was the best time to go. Because everything began to fall into place, finding a publisher, marketing strategy, and finally the endorsements.

I realized that just like everything else we have to go with God's time table, not our own. I just put my faith in God on how to proceed from the time I started the book until I received the last endorsement.

I thank God for giving me the desire to start this book and the strength to finish it. I had planned on retiring in June of 2016 so I could devote more time to my ministry and furthering the Kingdom of God. I kept thinking maybe I could put it off a month or so or maybe even next year. February 2016 the new owner (Ed's widow) called a company meeting and announced she was closing the company for good, effective March 2016. That took the question of when to retire completely out of my hands. Divine intervention? I think so.

I'm not writing this to say "hey look what I'm doing", I'm saying "hey look what God is doing!" I thank Him for the opportunity to serve Him and reach out to the ones who cannot otherwise be reached.

I tell this story to encourage others. Some are encouraged to know that you can be saved later in life...some think about a father, a husband, a wife knowing there is still a chance for them...age is not a factor.

There is this one young man I was talking to at a church in Cambria, California. Maybe late 20's or early 30's. When I told him my story his eyes teared up and he said… "Thank you so much, now I know there is hope for my father."

The Lord also led me to become an ordained chaplain which has opened more doors for serving Him in more ways.

So between my preaching, my book, and the chaplaincy, I truly believe God grabbed a hold of me when I was saved and said, "You've wasted enough time in your life, now I'm going to keep you running for Me, now get to work!"

At my age I no longer look back to see what I have done or what I haven't done. I look forward to see what needs to be done for the service of our Lord.

Chaplain Kathleen (Kali) Swope

Chaplain Kali grew up in a Catholic home, visited many times by priests, missionaries and nuns. Kali studied and worked in education. Her educational background is in Psychology and Communications. Her employment background included teaching High School juniors and seniors classes on a variety of self-help topics. After moving to Las Vegas she met and married her husband, Michael Zoccoli. Kali attends the International Church of Las Vegas Her current plans include volunteering with the Nevada Sex Trafficking Awareness Campaign.

In A Classroom

By Chaplain Kali Swope

I struggled several times in my life to achieve a loving relationship with my mother. As a child, I was difficult and tested her patience, and as an adult I did everything I could think of to earn her respect, forgiveness and ultimately her love. Another immense test came when my ex-husband decided to take our daughter out of my life. He was a strong and powerful man, who always got whatever he wanted. I had no money for a lawyer. Not one person could help me. I was alone.

So, I packed up and left my troubles behind, and moved to Las Vegas. Although I don't gamble, the Sin City is quite attractive with its luminosities and endless possibilities. For several years, I filled the void with alcohol and regret. Day after day seemed obscure, confused and without direction because I trusted me and only me. I glance back at that time and recall so many bad choices and a darkness that was completed with spiritual silence. But God said, "NO." I will end the era of self-pity and self-destruction.

While I was searching for answers, to my revelation, they were not revealed in the lights of Sin City, but in the people who showed me there was a smoldering flame inside of me; which could be ignited with God's compassion and love. I felt as if I was a child again, with all the burning passion and hunger for a new school of vigorous lessons and experiences.

Looking back, it seems as if the memories of disappointment, frustration, and hurt all lent themselves to the final outcome of life's learning lessons. What to do, what not to do…. "NO, don't do that." There are times it seems, life is like a classroom.

As a child, we understand the word NO long before we can walk or talk. There are times when God's answer to a prayer simply NO. Are we praying for something that will be bad for us? Bring us harm? Am I praying for candy and God gives me broccoli instead?

In our path of learning we experience evaluations and assessments every day. We step on the scale to assess our weight, the doctor evaluates our health and even our water is tested. A test in school is a calculation of what we know and what we need to spend more time learning. This gives us a visual to look at so we can work hard and change how we view the outcome.

Does God test me daily? Do I prepare for a test and where do I find the answers? Is it an assessment so I can see what I need to devote more time to learn?

I met my friend Barry soon after arriving in Sin City. We talked for hours and became friends. First, I just knew him as Barry, and then as Chaplain Barry. I wanted what he had. It reminded me of the toy every child wants for Christmas. You go to great lengths to obtain the toy and are overjoyed when you receive it. And then, you want the new and improved toy the following year. I pursued my faith lessons with the same enthusiasm. I felt my friend was a virtuous teacher and shepherd, he encouraged me to try harder, and he had faith in me and showed me the way. I was captivated by the Godly spiritual influence of his home church, and I was attracted to the way it changed my focus and feelings about so many things. I was baptized in Christ, and my friend Barry was there to support me.

Then, I met Jon. I volunteered to help him at church during the

 Christmas season and he gave me a copy of a book that he cherishes. At first, it looked just like every other daily devotional book, but this book included bible scriptures about what was relevant to the daily lessons. My parents never read from the bible, so my understanding was that the reading of scripture was only for clergy. I was not worthy, and someone like me would most likely, misinterpret the word of God. My Bible was on a book shelf, collecting dust, and only opened to record a birth or death in the family. Not anymore.

Jon was a teacher in the school of God's Word. An important first lesson I learned was to read the entire chapter before considering to quote the scripture. I might be missing the intended message if I take one verse out of context without knowing the entire meaning. So, in the quote below, if you open the Bible to the book of John and read chapter 15, you will see the complete reason why I chose verse 7. *"If you remain in me, and my words remain in you, ask whatever you wish and it will be done for you. John 15:7 (NIV)*

This lesson marked a vast change in how I view a daily test. If you have a test in school, the hardest is an essay test or something you have to memorize verbatim, but now I am a more confident test-taker because they are open book tests. I just open the Bible and the answers are in the Word.

All scripture is God-breathed and is useful for teaching, rebuking, correcting and training in righteousness so that the servant of God may be thoroughly equipped for very good work. 2Timothy 3: 16-17

The Lord's Prayer was my next course of study. The book of Matthew tells us about prayer, and for me, I studied this prayer one word at a time.

"....And forgive us our debts....." Matthew 6:12 (NIV)

I began to find answers for the test on forgiveness. Asking God to forgive me for the regrets that haunted me was a difficult undertaking. I know that to apologize sincerely, I must ask for forgiveness and make it right. With God, it is similar to say the words and repent with my actions. And then I can forgive myself. Then, it was a new struggle to take action with the next part of the prayer.

"....as we also have forgiven our debtors..." Matthew 6:12 (NIV)

I forgave my ex-husband and was at his side when he needed help moving and when he was sick. I understood that I had to soften my own heart or I could not learn to love again until I learned to forgive. God's plan with my mother was to lend one more lesson of forgiveness. I didn't think I could face any more pain but when she asked to see me before she died, I was on a plane, and spent every moment I could by my mother's side with my family. I'm not sure if she heard the things I said, or how she was feeling about forgiving me, only God truly knows that, at least for now.

I was holding my mother's hand, and praying with my niece when mom passed away. God was with me and, even though I was reminded of all the previous pain, ultimately I was at peace with all the good memories; which I created out of my love for her. Over and over again my strength was tested, and I either scored in passing, or with a failing grade. But these individual daily tests were specifically given to me, to see if I learned the lesson of forgiveness, in which I did.

I also learned that I was wasting my time on things that could have been, and I was not hearing the voice of God, nor seeing the good things on my new path.

In 2012, my husband and I lost our home, due in part, to the real estate crash in Las Vegas. Few of my personal possessions remain, and are locked away in a rented storage unit, and I live modestly in a small room. God knows what I need, and provides as described in the book of Matthew, chapter 6, and I do not worry.

"But seek first his kingdom and his righteousness, and all these things will be given to you as well. Therefore do not worry about tomorrow, for tomorrow will worry about itself." Matthew 6: 33-34

I would not listen to the voice of the enemy telling me I have no home, but I lifted up my cares to the Lord and I am safe in his powerful hands. God has me focused on today, not yesterday. What a joy it is to start every morning with a prayer, asking God to show me what He wants from me today. "Thy will be done…" is so much more delightful and productive. My life is simple now, and I have riches in love that I never imagined were possible. I am open to focus on God now, and my life is about serving Him, not a mortgage or other such burdens.

Remember the childhood celebrations when something went well? When you passed a big exam? When you were pleased with yourself? There was clapping, dancing and shouts of joy. As adults, we transform that to wiping the sweat off our brow, and saying that we are glad that it's over, whatever it may have been. Sometimes, we stop after simply saying, "Thank God." I take the time to rejoice, even for the little things, knowing that God is with me.

The overwhelming love of God began to surround me and hug me with a tenderness that was extraordinary, and trust was reestablished, like a child has an automatic trust when they are in the care of their parent; they are safe and secure, and that trust is the foundation of love. Trusting Father God brought tranquility back to my life.

"Trust in the Lord with all your heart and lean not on your own understanding; in all your ways submit to him, and he will make your paths straight." Proverbs 3: 5-6 (NIV)

I know that these lessons and many more were to prepare me. Similar to a rehearsal, where I can get a do-over until I get it right. A rehearsal or "re-hears-all" simply means I have another chance to re-hear, really listen, and receive what God has been saying me.

I believe it is part of God's plan to organize my future, and show me the path he has chosen for me. God says NO, when I fill my heart with regret. He reminds me that I am forgiven. God says NO, when I am lost, because he is always there to bring me back to the path, and gives me guidance. God says NO, when I am in a state of disbelief, and he strengthens my faith with love. I praise God for all the "yes's" in my life.

Today, I continue my journey with God's lesson plans on how I can reach out to others with His Word. One of my first steps is being a part of this book that allows me to witness His great love in my life. I humbly asked God for guidance to write some of my story, so that others can learn from my transparency. Many of you have felt the pain of loneliness and the feeling of being forgotten by man, but you are never forgotten by God.

May the Lord help you as He has helped me. May he show you your teachers, shepherds and faith family, and may my story help to make a difference and put a bounce in your footsteps. My cell phone contacts are filled with Messages of Faith Ministry Chaplains, who are rich in God's love. Ask yourself, who's in your cell phone contacts?

So, with this new day:

"This, then, is how you should pray:

Our Father in heaven, hallowed be your name, your kingdom come, your will be done, on earth as it is in heaven. Give us this day our daily bread. And forgive us our debts, as we also have forgiven our debtors. And lead us not into temptation, but deliver us from evil. Amen" Matthew 6: 9-13 (NIV)

Chaplain Warren Vandenhoff

Warren Vandenhoff is a CPE trained, ordained Christian Chaplain. He lives in Las Vegas, NV where he currently ministers as a hospital chaplain and a substance abuse counselor. In his thirty nine plus years of Christian ministry, he has held positions in Hawaii, California, New York and Nevada in hospital ministry, prayer ministry, prison ministry, homeless ministry, substance abuse ministry; and has served in cross cultural Christian missions to numerous Pacific Rim countries.

Reflections from the Threshing Floor

By Chaplain Warren Vandenhoff

We can be strengthened and filled with greater courage when we know we are not alone. Kathryn Kuhlman[i] once stated " the secret of victory over fear is very simple – it is trusting Jesus!" One of the most frequent expressions on His lips throughout His life here on earth was, "Fear not!" So look up! Faith in God has in times past "subdued kingdoms, wrought righteousness, obtained promises, stopped the mouths' of lions, quenched the violence of fire, escaped the edge of the sword…turned to flight the armies of the aliens" (Hebrews 11:33, 34), and FAITH CAN DO IT AGAIN! You are not only a conqueror; you can be more than a conqueror through Him Who loves you!

Amen to that. You may ask can I be brave like the soaring eagle that flies head first into the approaching thunderstorm, instinctively hitting that invisible updraft that will carry him on his magnificent outstretched wings up, up and above the menacing thick black clouds to an altitude filled with blue skies and abundant light. I wonder if he closes his eyes while doing this, how any clear vision can be had with the velocity and force of air streaming into the bird's face is beyond my understanding. But then again, didn't our Lord ask us to consider another bird, the sparrows, in Luke 12:7? "I tell you, my friends, do not be afraid of those who kill the body and after that can do no more. But I will show you whom you should fear.

179

Fear Him who after the killing of the body has power to throw you into hell. Yes, I tell you fear him. Are not five sparrows sold for two pennies? Yet not one of them is forgotten by God. Indeed the very hairs on your head are all numbered. Don't be afraid, you are worth more than many sparrows. I tell you, whoever acknowledges me before men, the Son of Man will also acknowledge him before the angels of God." This sounds like pretty good company to me, is it really attainable? And if so how and where?

Maybe the answer to that can be found in the lyrics of this song[ii] written by Melissa Helser,

"I heard about a threshing floor
Where Gideon saw the Angel of the Lord
I wanna go there and be with You

I heard about a secret place
Where Moses went and saw Your face
I wanna go there, and be with You

Take me home
To the place where I belong
There's nothing that I want more
than the presence of the Lord

I heard about an upper room
Where tongues of fire fall on you
I wanna go there, and be with You

I heard about this garden where
You and man walk hand in hand
I wanna go there and be with You

Take me home
To the place where I belong

There's nothing that I want more
than the Presence of the Lord

I heard about a threshing floor
Where Gideon saw the Angel of the Lord
I wanna go there and be with You "

A threshing floor is a smooth, flat surface that was used in the process of harvesting grain.[iii] Before there was machinery, farmers used a threshing floor to separate the grain from the chaff. The harvested produce would be spread over the threshing floor and then animals (cattle or oxen) would be led over it, to crush and break the sheaves apart with their hooves. At times, people used sticks to beat the sheaves apart (Ruth 2:17; Isaiah 28:27). The grain would be separated from the husks, or chaff (Deuteronomy 25:4; Isaiah 28:28) and then tossed into the air so that the wind could blow the chaff away, leaving only the good, edible grain. This was called "winnowing."

A threshing floor[iv] is important in the biblical story of Ruth and Boaz. In those times, if a woman's husband died, it was very difficult for her to survive on her own, and very often, the woman would be "redeemed" by her husband's nearest kinsmen (Leviticus 25:25; Ruth 2:20). Ruth was encouraged by her mother-in-law, Naomi, to go down to the threshing floor where Boaz was winnowing barley. She was to wait until he had finished eating and drinking and was lying down for the night, and then uncover his feet and lay down at his feet, for this was a symbol of her desire to be redeemed by Boaz. The connection between the kinsmen redeemer and the threshing floor in this story is likely not incidental.

The threshing floor is symbolic of judgment in the Bible. Old Testament prophet Hosea prophesied that Israel would be "like the morning mist or like the dew that goes early away, like the chaff that swirls from the threshing floor or like smoke from a window" (Hosea 13:3). Of the nations who will come against God during the end times, the prophet Micah says "they do not know the thoughts of the Lord; they do not understand his plan, that he has gathered them as sheaves to the threshing floor." The idea is that Israel will demolish their enemies like oxen trampling grain on the threshing floor" (Micah 4:11-13). Chaff is referred to in the Psalms as a symbol of the destruction of the wicked (Psalm 1:4). Also, John the Baptist referred to Jesus as the one who would separate the good grain from the chaff with a winnowing fork, gathering the grain into his barn and burning the chaff with "unquenchable fire" (Matthew 3:12). This is a symbol of heaven and hell.

The threshing floor has spiritual significance as the place where good and evil are separated. Ruth symbolizes the believer, or spiritual Israel, for she was a Gentile who converted to Judaism (Ruth 1:16). Boaz is a symbol of Christ—the Redeemer. When Ruth comes to the threshing floor she is in need, and has responded to Boaz's previous kindness and generosity (Ruth 2:8-13). She has learned that he is a good man, and she trusts him. The fact that her petition takes place at the threshing floor, among the grain and the chaff, is a beautiful symbol of man's need for redemption and God's identity as Redeemer (Job 19:25; Psalm 19:14; Psalm 78:35). The difference between the grain and the chaff, between good and evil people, is not their good or evil works. The grain is gathered into the barn by faith, by the gift of God, who provides righteousness and spiritual safety through Jesus Christ, our kinsmen Redeemer (Romans 1:17; Romans 3:22-24; Hebrews 2:11-15).

To trust God in hard times Christians must surrender to God and submit to the Word of God. Partnering with trust is the concept of surrender, a term usually associated with defeat. Its usage here, however, means that a believer completely gives up his own will and subjects his thoughts, ideas and deeds to the Word and will of God. Surrendering to God is simply another way of saying submitting completely to Him.

In Luke 18:18-23, a wealthy man came to Jesus and asked him, *"What shall I do to inherit eternal life?"* Jesus recited five of the Ten Commandments to him, and the man replied, *"All these things I have kept from my youth."* Then Jesus said, *"You still lack one thing. Sell all that you have and distribute to the poor, and you will have treasure in heaven; and come, follow Me."*

When the man heard this, he became very sad, because he was very rich. This man was sincere, and was conscientious about obedience to the commandments. But he loved his money more than God, and was not ready to give it up for treasure in heaven. His priority of immediate earthly comfort blinded his eyes to any future consequences.

Often times it takes times of crises to awaken people to what is truly valuable in life. God's Word differentiates for believers what is lasting and meaningful, and what is not. *"Do not love the world or the things in the world. If anyone loves the world, the love of the Father is not in him. For all that is in the world -- the lust of the flesh, the lust of the eyes, and the pride of life is not of the Father but is of the world. And the world is passing away, and the lust of it; but he who does the will of God abides forever."* (1 John 2:15-17)

The threshing floor in the bible is symbolic for purification.[1] When you begin your threshing floor experience you may feel as if you have been through so much you can't go on. You may be at a point where you are on your knees crying out to God to rescue you. You probably want this time of trial in your life to just end. You are at a crossroads with God and it's either go on with Him or go back into the world. As you raise your hands to God and surrender all to Him a beautiful thing is about to happen in your life. You are going to experience the end of sitting on the threshing floor and waiting. You are being prepared to enter the Holy Of Holies and God is going to meet you there and you will walk in supernatural intimacy with God that you have only dreamed of prior to this day.

So many people today are going through some of the hardest times they have ever known. Things that they have built a lifetime around have been snatched from them. They don't understand and none of us ever understands why trials and tribulations come. One thing is for sure, if you can hold on tighter than ever to God and press into him tightly your life will never be the same. Yes, deliverance is found there along with your freedom from the fowler's snare. Our Redeemer will break every chain.

Now let's consider Revival. In the Bible the definitive book and verse about Revival is 2 Chronicles 7:14. " If my people who are called by My name humble themselves, pray and seek My face, and turn from their evil ways, then I will hear from heaven, forgive their sin, and heal their land." It is addressed to those called by God's name, and it presents a 4/3 formula for revival.

THE REQUIREMENTS FOR REVIVAL

Humble yourselves. Pride is a beaver's dam that holds back the currents of personal and corporate revival.

Pray. History's great revivals have been prayed down by burdened souls.

Seek His Face. Get serious about your relationship with Christ and the spiritual habits that draw us closer to Him.

Turn from our wicked ways. If we are doing anything careless, immoral, or disobedient, we must confess it and reestablish obedience to that area of life.

THE PROMISES OF REVIVAL

I will hear from heaven. God will listen to our prayers as carefully as He listened to Solomon's in 2 Chronicles 6.

I will forgive their sin. God specializes in forgiveness. There is not a sin on earth that He will not instantly and permanently forgive when sincerely confessed and placed under the blood of the cross.

I will heal their land. Has any land needed healing more urgently than ours? Has any generation needed revival more than this one?

There is a significant relationship with Revival and The Threshing Floor Experience. Let's unpack the meaning of The Threshing Floor again, grasp its meaning, personally find it, live it daily and share it with others.

As said previously and it deserves repeating, the threshing floor in the Bible is symbolic for purification. When you begin your threshing floor experience you may feel as if you have been through so much you can't go on. You may be at a point where you are on your knees crying out to God to rescue you. You probably want this time of trial in your life to just end. You are at a crossroads with God and it's either go on with Him or go back into the world. As you raise your hands to God and surrender all to Him a beautiful thing is about to happen in your life. You are going to experience the end of sitting on the threshing floor and waiting. You are being prepared to enter the Holy Of Holies and God is going to meet you there and you will walk in a supernatural intimacy with God that you have only dreamed of prior to this day. One thing is for sure, if you can hold on tighter than ever to God and press into him tightly your life will never be the same.

As hard as it is this is the time to say to God, just as Job did, that you don't understand why this has happened but nevertheless you still intend to lift your hands and praise His name.

This is the time to go into your prayer closet with God and take a good look at your life so far. What is the one thing that you have been having a hard time giving to God? Is it your attitude? Is it your critical tongue, gossiping, drugs, drinking, sex addiction? What ever it is this is when the time is ripe for God to begin to thresh it out of your life. It may be the last stronghold that Satan has over your soul. God is going to thresh out that "thing" and He is going to keep threshing until He separates you "the wheat" from the "chaff" of sin.

The threshing floor experience is not pleasant but looking back on it, it is the one time in my life that I realized that He was all I needed. I could relax and be happy within the intimate relationship established between God and me. In that intimacy with the Lord a quiet trust grew. I know that through whatever storms my life might bring I have a safe harbor to rest in with the Lord.

We know that after wheat goes through the threshing process it is then ready to be used. This is the way it is with us. After going through this process we pass through to another level with the Lord. Now being ready for His purposes we can minister to others who find themselves on the threshing floor. If you are going through the threshing process today you are blessed. You see, the Father loves you so much that He wants to spend quality time with you. He wants to use this time to separate the wheat from the chaff in your life because He has something for you to do. He sees that you are worthy of taking time with because He knows what He has planned for the end product of your life. God is our master builder, press forward and find him .All progress takes place outside the comfort zone, we are alive to Praise Him.

Chaplain Duey Vernon

Duey Vernon is a native of Henderson, NV. Duey and his wife have 7 children, 11 grandchildren and 1 great grandchild. While Duey has made a living as an electrical contractor, he has also enjoyed his volunteer time of 4 years with the National Park Service and 33 years with the Police Auxiliary Civilian team where he worked his way up to the position of Chief. He now devotes most of his free time riding his motorcycle with the Christian Motorcyclist Association and serves as the local Chaplain. Duey is an ordained Chaplain with Chaplaincy Nevada. The story you will read by Duey Vernon is a testimony of God's ability to turn a bad situation into a tool to spread the good news with. Duey has shared this story to churches and youth groups and plans to continue to tell everyone that will listen about a modern-day miracle.

Bullet of Faith

By Chaplain Duey Vernon

I will always remember the day that I was so close to getting my first full drum set. I had been a drummer in the school marching band and because of my stocky size; I was usually the one carrying the bass drum. My friend from church and I had been working on my parents for a couple of weeks to buy his used drum set. So when my parents told me that we were going to go visit my friend's family, I thought we had made progress. I was suspicious that it was not just a visit because we had never visited them at their home before, so I was very hopeful that I might be getting that drum set for my soon to come birthday. As we were getting ready to go to their home I got cleaned up, put on fresh clothes and my new shoes so I would look my best.

On that day, May 5th, 1975, being thirteen, I remember thinking that this was going to be a special day because my favorite number was 5 and so it must mean that I was going to get that much desired drum set. As our car turned the corner from Lamb Blvd. onto Cheyenne Ave. in Las Vegas, a drunken man shot at our car. Later we learned that he was aiming for the back tire, so the car would stop and he could get in it for a ride to the Wagon Wheel Saloon to get more beer. The 30.06 went through the car in front of the right rear tire, slicing through my sister's dress, scratching her back on both sides of her spine and through my right thigh. Next it traveled under my left leg because my left foot was on the hump in the floor and then into the front seat hitting my dad's back at his belt.

I felt a bump at the same time I heard a loud bang and my thought was that my Dad had ran over a rock. I looked down and saw that my right thigh was three times its normal size, my jeans and skin had ripped open, so my next thought was that my Dad had ran over a rock and my thigh had fallen apart. I screamed out and my father pulled the car over. My father knew right away that I had been shot and that it was not a rock because we were driving in a desert area and he thought that someone had accidentally shot in our direction. As he got out of the car he opened the back door to see if he needed to put a tourniquet on my leg. Just then he saw a man step out from behind the bushes and point a riffle at him. He quickly jumped back into the car. As my Dad took off he yelled, "Everyone get down, he's shooting at us". My sister slid down onto the floor and I laid to my right behind her. My mother and brother were in the front seat and they slid down as far as they could.

He drove quickly, swerving in the dirt to kick up a dust cloud to make it harder to see us in case he was going to shoot at us again. As we sped toward the North Las Vegas Hospital my Dad was flashing his headlights and honking his horn. A North Las Vegas Police Officer saw this and knew we were going in the direction of the hospital. He then turned on his lights and siren, and sped in front of our car helping us to get to the hospital faster. I don't think you would see this happen today but our family is grateful that this officer had the mindset to help us get there and then ask "why" later.

As I laid there in the back seat I remembered watching one of my favorite TV shows called Emergency. On that show they had an episode where a boy had been bitten by a snake. They told him to relax because it would slow down his heart beat so the venom would take longer to travel to the heart. I now believe God allowed me to watch that show to prepare me for that moment in the back seat of my Dad's car after being shot by a drunken man. So I did just that, I relaxed as much as I could even though I thought I was bleeding out right there in the back seat. I later learned that if the bullet, the bullet fragments or any of the sharp bone edges had nicked the artery then I would have had only four and one half minutes to live.

We were nine minutes away from the hospital. If you don't think you have ever seen or heard of a miracle happening in today's time, let me assure you that this was a miracle. Just picture in your mind the bone in your thigh. It's called the Femur or the Femur Shaft and it is the longest and strongest bone in your body. Running along the Femur Shaft are both the Femoral Artery and the Femoral Vein. So the first miracle was that several inches of bone were fractured into countless pieces leaving me with not only fractured bone pieces but also bullet fragments. This tore up about six inches of muscle and made it look like "meatloaf". The very hand of God shielded the vital artery and vein. The second miracle was the two fragments of the bullet that had traveled up my thigh and around my stomach area for over two feet each. The miracle here is that the surgeon could see the path of destruction and stated that he could see that as they approached vital organs they each would turn to avoid them. He told my mother that those two fragments should have killed me faster and could have been more dangerous than what had happened to my leg.

After I calmed myself down I then started to pray. I started my prayer as "No, not me God, not me!" But then I said "Wait, I'm ready God; if this is my time then I am ready. Please take care of my Mother and my family, I am ready if it is your plan but if it is at all possible, I would like to continue living on earth to live long enough to raise a family of my own as a Christian family".

When we arrived at the hospital they pulled my sister out of the car and It seemed to take forever for them to get me out. I'm sure it wasn't as long as I thought but I remember thinking that I didn't want my leg to fall the rest of the way off as they pulled my body out and I'm sure they were cautious as well. I kept saying that my stomach was hurting, over and over. I didn't feel any pain from my leg. Later I found out there was a good reason it hurt with those two fragments traveling around in there. The hospital staff, family and friends gathered in a prayer circle outside the surgery room. The hospital had contacted two surgeons, one for my leg and one for my stomach. The leg surgeon, who had practiced in Vietnam, came in and started cleaning my leg for amputation as he had done so many times before. However, an idea came to him that because I was young and still growing, my leg could grow back together. I am told that he brought up the idea with the other Vietnam experienced surgeon. He continued to clean up the leg for several hours and then braced me to a bed with weights attached to the lower part of my leg.

Today I walk on my own without any pins or brackets in my leg. It is a little shorter than my left leg and I am sure that has contributed to my back problems. My parents were told that I would be in ICU for 48 hours, then after two months in a hospital bed I would be in a body cast at home for three more months. After about twelve hours they brought me out of the ICU and I walked out of that hospital on crutches after only two months and without any body cast at all.

Years later, when I was 18 and working at a department store called Woolco, a co-worker named Howard and I figured out that we were part of the same story. He told me that he was in the trailer park just North of Cheyenne Ave. on Lamb Blvd. on May 5th, because someone had posted an ad to sell a mobile home. He had heard some of the details and this is what he told me; On that day, there was a man that had been drinking and ran out of beer. He told his wife to go get him some more beer, but she knew that he had been drinking way too much already so she took the kids and the keys to the car and went to a neighbor's house. After a little while he realized that his wife was not showing up with more beer so he went to see if he could find his own way to get more alcohol. He started walking down the street when he saw a motorcycle in a neighbor's driveway with a lock on it. So he went back into his house to retrieve his 30.06 rifle and came out and shot the lock off. He then tried to kick start the motorcycle but it wouldn't start. He then started to walk down the street with the rifle when he approached Howard and the other man talking about the sale of a mobile home. The drunken man decided to point the rifle at them and said that if you're chicken you'll run. Howard thought it might be a nutty friend of the seller until he saw that the seller was running. Howard jumped over a fence and a lady on the other side opened her door to see what the shooting was about and Howard ran in.

The drunken gunman then proceeded to leave the trailer park and head out on foot to get his beer. He stumbled toward the corner of Cheyenne Ave. and Lamb Blvd. When he got to the corner he saw a car approaching so he hid behind a bush. That just happened to be our car. As our car passed by him he shot at the back tire. I am guessing that he was trying to account for lead time on a moving car because he shot just ahead of the tire. The problem with this theory is that he was only ten to fifteen feet away and using a 30.06 rifle. The good thing was that he was already too drunk to think straight and if he had aimed a few inches to his left and hit the tire then when the bullet entered the car it would have missed my sister and then ripped right through my hips instead of my thigh. The miracles just kept happening. As my father was driving away in an attempt to save my life, another car came along and this time the gunman just stood in the road pointing the rifle at the car until the car came to a stop. The gunman then got into the back seat of the car with an elderly couple and told them to drive him to a saloon nearby. Just at that moment a police officer, that had already stopped by the mobile home park looking for him and was directed to the desert by others at the park, was coming down the road and saw the gunman get into the car. The officer followed them to the saloon on Nellis Dr. and walked up to the car shoving his shotgun into the side of the gunman's head and arrested him.

I had been telling this story for years when I found out that there was more to the story. In April of 1975, my mother and 11-year-old sister were in the kitchen baking some cookies when my 7-year-old brother (who had been watching TV) came into the kitchen ranting about something he had seen on TV. His rant was that if someone was to hurt anyone in our family then we would go rough them up. My sister abruptly stopped what she was doing and in a matter-a-fact tone, she told her little brother that if something happens to someone in our family that we pray about it and God will take care of everything. My mother just stood there looking at my sister and then looked up. As it says in Proverbs 1:33 (NASB), "But he who listens to me shall live securely, and will be at ease from the dread of evil". She knew that God had just spoken to her, she didn't know when or what, but she knew that in a crisis it would turn out OK. She told me many years later about what had happened in the kitchen and I too know that he had warned my mother to give her peace of mind and heart at that time.

I have had people ask me how I could believe in a God when he would LET something like this happen to me. I just tell them that he did not LET this happen to me but that I had prayed for something like this to happen to me. Let me explain...I grew up with a father that is a minister. He was and is a very smart man that could get up on that platform and explain the bible and what it meant to just about anyone. I was the kid with ADD and the very bad grades in school and I was always praying to God for help to be able to share his word. I thought you had to get good grades and be very smart to share God with others. When I was shot and lived through it I realized that I was a living testimony for God. He had answered my prayers and gave me a way to share my story with many people. I believe that God still performs miracles every day. It is important to ask ourselves; Am I a walking testimony for God? I give you permission to use my story until you become conscious of your own because they really are all God's stories. He can turn our tests into testimonies.

So thank you for reading my testimony and just in case you were wondering...no, I never did get a drum set.

Is God Calling You To Be An Author?

If you feel like God is calling you to be an author or you are not sure answer these questions. Find yourself a journal, notebook or a simple clean sheet of paper. Get still and be present and pray for God"s insight and revelation to help you answer these questions. After you thoroughly answer these questions, sincerely and in full participation, God will reveal the answer.

1. For the already published writers, write the titles of your books, blogs, and magazine articles. If you are not published yet leave this space for last after you have completed the rest of the questions. Let the Holy Spirit give you an inspired book, chapter, blog post or article title.

2. Write your writer's resume – what have you written whether its published or not.

3. Write your Bio

- Personal (non work related accomplishment you've done)

- Professional

4. Where have you traveled?

5. What do you do in your free time?

6. What are your hobbies?

7. What are the last five books you read (completely)?

8. What are your top five books to recommend to secular friends?

9. What are your top five books to recommend to Christian Friends?

10. What is your favorite movie?

11. What is your favorite Christian movie?

12. What's your favorite scripture?

Write what this scripture means to you (in 100 words or less)

Thank you for completing these questions. If you would like to talk about your answers and pursue writing your story and sharing your testimony, please contact me ChaplainTamia@gmail.com. You have experienced all you have experienced for such a time as this. Help someone else see how God worked it out for your good.

Blessings of abundant Faith,

Tamia Dow

Senior Chaplain Message of Faith Ministries

On Facebook - Chaplain Dow

On Twitter - @chaplaindow

By email – ChaplainTamia@gmail.com

www.tamiadow.com

Special Thanks:

Editing Team
Dorla Stewart, Alvin Weesner, Beverly Weesner, Tamia Dow

Review Team
Sally StJohn, Victorya, Tamia Dow, Debbie Damron,

Formatting Team
Victorya and Tamia Dow

Faith Is, the gift that keeps on giving, from Chaplaincy Nevada.

If you are in need of prayer please contact us at
chaplainsprayer@gmail.com

Please visit us on-line at:

www.messagesoffaith.net

www.chaplaincynevada.org

Thank you for purchasing this anthology.

All proceeds from this book go to assisting the Chaplaincy
Fundraising team, and Nevada Chaplains in their trainings and
outreaches.

Be on the look out for our next anthology coming later in 2017.

The Lord Bless You and Keep You
The Lord Make His Face Shine On You
And Be Gracious To You
The Lord Turn His Face Toward You
And Give You Peace
Numbers 6:24-26

Made in the USA
Columbia, SC
22 December 2019